Now you tell me!

12
COLLEGE
STUDENTS
GIVE THE
BEST ADVICE
THEY NEVER
GOT

SHERIDAN SCOTT
NANCY ALLEN • ANYA SETTLE

Arundel Publishing
P.O. Box 377
Warwick, NY 10990
www.arundelpublishing.com
www.nowyoutellmebooks.com

ISBN 978-1-933608-26-6
First Edition May 2012
Printed in the United States of America.

TABLE OF CONTENTS

Ben Allen	1
Anya Settle	11
Kelly Fleming	25
Imani Finn	39
Thomas Groneman	47
Mallory Craig	57
Joshua Tanis	67
Catherine Raleigh	77
Benjamin Pearce	89
Aislinn Ryan	97
Lucas Paez	107
Nicole Barron	117
Bonus Material	127
Jane Adams	129
Kaleen Long	139
Angela Webber	149
Stress-Free Transitioning to College: How Parents Can Help	153
Stuff You Should Bring	161
About the Authors	169

BEN ALLEN

"College will give you a larger understanding of the world."

B en began his college career at Oklahoma State University and later transferred to Missouri State University. He has learned how to negotiate the delicate balance between sleep aids and caffeine and that there will be professors who change your life forever, and those that seem to only make your life more difficult. A fraternity member, political science major, self-proclaimed CollegeHumor.com enthusiast, and recent graduate, Ben plans to continue his education in law school.

COLLEGE LEARNING

CHOOSING A SCHOOL

When it was time to pick a college, I chose Oklahoma State University in Stillwater, Oklahoma. It was the right school for a number of reasons; I knew I wanted to go out of state—get away from the hometown—and OSU was five hours away, which seemed about right. I was truly on my own but could get home if I had to. And even though Stillwater is a little town, it has easy access to a big city, Tulsa, which is only sixty miles down the interstate. I liked the look of OSU, too—the visual appearance; the architectural uniformity of the campus is amazing. And the people there are remarkably friendly.

> **There's nothing that will set a base, a foundation, for a satisfying college experience like a social network that is comprised of people who are genuine friends.**

But without a doubt, the most important factor for my enthusiasm for OSU was the fraternity I joined. There's nothing that will set a base, a foundation, for a satisfying college experience like a social network that is comprised of people who are genuine friends.

Before I paint too rosy a picture of college life, I should be frank about some of the perils and pitfalls of the freshman year. As an incoming freshman just out of high school, you've got to understand that you are responsible for yourself now. You're an adult, and that means that you have to make adult choices about the college life.

CHOOSING A MAJOR

I changed my major three times, from education to business to political science. Changing your major isn't a problem; but it can add to the amount of time, the number of semesters you spend in undergraduate school.

If you get all your general education requirements out of the way first, that gives you some time to grow up a little bit; and that helps as far as picking a major goes. How many people know exactly how they want to spend the rest of their lives within a few short weeks of finishing high school? But that's what picking a major the first semester entails. Taking the required college courses introduces you to different areas of study, and you'll be able to better figure out which degree program is a good fit for you.

So now I'm a political science major, and I plan to go to law school after graduation. I like poli sci because I want to know about the world around me, how it functions, and what to do when it does not. This drives me. This is why I majored in political science.

GOOD PROFESSORS

My first semester at OSU, I enrolled in a class that wasn't in my area; I was just taking one of my general ed requirements, and I encountered a professor who was a genius. He inspired me. He was actually able to change the way people thought. Students who had come to college confident in their worldview, secure in the righteousness of their personal beliefs, would be challenged by this man. He had tremendous charisma and an incredible intellect, and he was able to open our minds to new thoughts about ethics and morality and the world in which we live. Whenever he spoke, we would all listen. There was nobody in that class who didn't leave changed because of him. No one who didn't have a larger understanding of the world. He did amazing things.

ONLINE COURSES

When you sign up for an Internet course, even though your friends assure you that it's a mindless class that will fulfill a gen ed requirement with no effort on your part, beware of their advice. Don't go into the course with the idea that you can forget about it all semester and then you'll be able to complete all of the assignments within the last seventy-two hours of the semester. 'Cause you can't. Believe me.

PULLING ALL-NIGHTERS

I pulled a few all-nighters, I admit, and I don't recommend the practice. For one thing, when you stay up all night, you feel "zombiefied" the next morning. You'll either skip your morning classes or you'll sleep through them; either way, it's a bad academic practice.

> **If you have to stay up all night to prepare for a class, whether to study for an exam or finish a paper or project, you're doing something wrong.**

If you have to stay up all night to prepare for class, whether to study for an exam or to finish a paper or project, you're doing something wrong. You need to rethink how you are scheduling your study time.

STUDY HABITS

Don't take sleep aids. I'm talking about the over-the-counter sleep inducers. They'll make you sleep through your morning classes. I had suite mates who were gamers; and they stayed up playing and talking into the early hours of the morning, day after day, night after night. I couldn't sleep, so I gave the sleep aids a try—and I do NOT recommend them.

SKIPPING CLASS

Skipping class is not a good idea. It's hard to resist sometimes, though, when you're a gamer with a new game or in need of catching some extra ZZZs.

Another pitfall to avoid is the temptation to skip when you've aced the first exam. Even if the first test demonstrated that the course is a breeze for you, don't assume that you've got the class nailed down. In one class I fell victim to the notion that I didn't need to go to class to do well because I had a good grasp of the subject matter and the answers to the exam questions came easily to me. Just when you think you've got an A in the bag, they trip you up with quizzes or attendance points. Take it from one who knows: you have to go to class to perform well in the course.

TRANSFERRING

I eventually transferred to the state university in my hometown. It happens. And when it does, a transfer to another college is not the end of the world. It's best to look at it as the beginning of something new.

There are lots of reasons why people transfer: finances, academics, relationships, roommates. Did you storm out of your biology class, never to return? Did you miss your girlfriend too much? Did you sleep through one too many morning classes?

When you transfer, you may have to leave some things behind. The college I transferred to didn't have a chapter of my fraternity at OSU, and I missed that. It was also sad to leave the collection of friends I'd made there. But, when you're returning to your home base, you may not need a social fraternity as much.

You are not confined to one single, perfect match in education; there are many fine schools out there, just like there's more than one compatible person in life.

The fact is, there are many institutions that will equip you for your life after college. You can transfer to another college and proceed smoothly toward your goal. You are not confined to one single, perfect match in education; there are many fine schools out there, just like there's more than one compatible person in life.

COLLEGE LIFE

FREEDOM

One of the greatest gifts of the college experience can also be a curse: FREEDOM. You are free to do what you want when you want, go where you want, eat what you want . . . I could go on, but you get the point. All that freedom. Watch out!

DORM ROOM ESSENTIALS

Dorm rooms are very Spartan. The university will only provide you with a small bed and an old desk—only the very basics for existence. Everyone has individual necessities: some people can't live without ice-cold soda, or coffee, or microwave popcorn. Bear in mind that you will probably have to provide your own refrigerator, microwave, and coffeemaker to enjoy these luxuries.

You know you need an alarm clock in college. Everyone will tell you that. But choosing an alarm clock with a snooze button is crucial. I find that you should set your alarm with sufficient time to hit the snooze a couple or three times before you really have to get up. I like to set it for an hour before I have to get to class because it gives me time to mentally prepare myself to get out of bed.

A laptop and a printer are a great help, and I definitely recommend that you bring your own equipment from home. The college will have computer labs on campus, and it's handy to know where they are, even if you have your own equipment, in the event of a technological breakdown when you're in the midst of an important paper and you're working on a deadline.

Choosing an alarm clock with a snooze button is crucial.

Headphones are a necessity. When three diverse people are occupying the same living space, it's pivotal that you be able to block out distractions of music, television, gaming, etc.

Family photos are extremely important. Every day when you get up, the photos remind you not only who's paying for your education, but also who's counting on you to do your best. That should energize you.

A coffeemaker is a necessary part of college. You'll learn to drink coffee, even if you've never tried it before; and odds are, you'll learn to love it. There's something civilized and bracing about enjoying a cup of hot coffee on a college campus.

I would warn, though, against the overuse of caffeinated products such as energy drinks. While some may write it off as urban legend, the reality is that too much caffeine is bad for you; and if you have heart issues, you should be cautious about the results of getting too wired on caffeine. I pulled an all-nighter fueled on coffee and energy drinks, and I ended up at the student health center with chest pains.

DAY-TO-DAY LIFE

Cleaning. Oftentimes, roommates will prove to have different cleaning priorities, and the dorm room will soon be in disarray. Early on I dealt with the disorder by refusing to pick up anything or clean anything until the other people I lived with initiated the cleanup first. If they didn't clean, I didn't clean.

This created problems. When you live in a pile of discarded clothes and trash, things disappear. I could not find things—important things, sometimes. Such as my cell phone. My car keys. Flash drives that contained reports and speeches. That was probably the worst.

Take my advice: keep your room and belongings in reasonable order.

Laundry. My mother was my laundress for the first eighteen years of my life, and it took some adjustment when I went to college and her services disappeared. The laundry process seems complex at times: sure, you've always got the dirty clothes, but to wash them you're required to have detergent. And quarters: lots and lots of quarters. Which means you can't do laundry if you're broke, or even if you have no access to a money changer.

BEN'S LIFE DISCOVERIES

- When you run into the Taco Bell, even though you're only going in for a minute, take your keys. Particularly, don't lock your only set of keys in the car with the engine running.

- If you don't do your laundry, what you save in quarters you will lose in clothing options. When you have to choose between the ketchup stain and the mustard stain, it complicates your life.

- Dorm food sucks. Except for the vanilla pudding.

So I found that I was washing my clothes weekly. Then later, maybe every two weeks. But what you save in quarters you lose in clothing options. When you have to choose between the ketchup stain and the mustard stain, it complicates your life.

Sleeping. I love to sleep. I'm happy sleeping until 11:00 a.m. or so. And then there's the afternoon nap. I'm a believer in the siesta.

The downside to all this sleeping, of course, is that you're ignoring the responsibility you have, the duty to go to class and to study. It's hard to get to those morning classes when you are sleeping till noon, and you're in danger of snoozing through the afternoon classes when the siesta runs on too long. When you pursue your own structure for the day and ignore the obligations of college, there's a price to pay.

I no longer indulge in the siesta. It was nice while it lasted, though.

Eating dorm food. It's a cliché, but I'll say it anyway: dorm food sucks. Except for the vanilla pudding. I ate vanilla pudding every day.

Because I think it's important to keep an open mind, I sampled any number of the entrées and menu offerings at the dorm but was invariably disappointed. At breakfast the scrambled eggs tasted like they came from a carton, not from a shell, so I ate cereal. At lunch and dinner I ate spaghetti. Every day. And vanilla pudding.

The downside of a diet of pasta and vanilla pudding is that a person may run into nutritional deficiencies. Fortunately, I discovered Flintstones vitamins.

WHEN YOU GET SICK . . .

Though you may firmly believe that you'll never be homesick and that the absence of your hovering parents will never sadden you, just wait till you get sick at college. Compared to your housing at college, your parents' home was a sanitized environment. Dorms and Greek houses are petri dishes for flu and colds and strep throat, and sooner or later you will get sick. You'll get hit by a bug. Though being five hours away from your parents is awesome on most levels, there is nothing worse in college than being sick in your dorm.

If you need medical attention, every college has a health center where you can go to see a doctor (also helpful to provide documentation for missing class). And they won't let you starve at college; during the swine flu pandemic, food was delivered to sick students by staff in HazMat suits.

As for ways to avoid it, you could scrub your room regularly and toil with a variety of cleansers in a futile attempt to keep down the bacteria count. But would that make your college experience better? If the answer is no, then throw down that mop, and pick up that Xbox 360 console, and play some Halo: Reach on Xbox LIVE.

CAR KEYS

Just an aside: when you run into the Taco Bell, even though you're only going in for a minute, take your keys. Make sure they're in your pocket or your hand. Don't lock them in the car. And particularly, don't lock your only set of keys in the car with the engine running. Bear in mind that your family is five hours away; they can't come rushing to the rescue with a spare key.

AND MOST IMPORTANTLY . . .

Four years of college will change the way you see the world. There is no getting around it. College will change you in ways that no other place will or ever could. You're simply exposed to so many different ideas and concepts by so many enlightened people, it can't help but alter you. College will change your worldview in some way—maybe completely. You will see the world around you through new eyes. ★

For more from Ben go to
www.nowyoutellmebooks.com/college.

ANYA SETTLE

"Illegitimis non carborundum. Seriously."

Originally from San Diego, California, Anya defined her college career at Dickinson College by her involvement in the arts. She was a member of a coed a capella group, contributed to the school's literary magazine, and participated as one of two student poets at the international Semana Poética poetry festival, which allowed her to connect with her own Mexican heritage. She graduated Phi Beta Kappa with a BA in English, a minor in creative writing, and several new tattoos.

BEFORE YOU LEAVE

Pack light. You don't need to bring as much stuff with you as you think you do. Chances are, you won't need it all; and if you find that you need something that you left behind, you can always make a quick trip to the campus store or a nearby convenience or department store. I brought two SUVs, both packed to the roof with stuff on my freshman move-in day and found that I didn't use half of it. Being selective with what you choose to bring, and sticking to the essentials, will leave you with much more space, which in and of itself is an essential when living in a dorm.

With that being said, don't leave behind inessential items simply because they are inessential. You may not *need* pictures of friends and family, stuffed animals, artwork or other decorations; but if they make you happy or make your room more comfortable, bring them. Your dorm room will be your home for nine months, so bring what you must and do what you must in order to make it into something that's not merely livable, but that will actually *feel* like home.

Meet your roommate. Once I was accepted to Dickinson and verified that I would be attending, I was asked to fill out a questionnaire detailing my sleeping and study habits, tidiness, whether or not I was a smoker, and so on and so forth. I was assigned a roommate based on my answers. My roommate and I got in touch right away and even had the opportunity to meet several weeks before school started. A close friend who happened to live near my roommate had a party, and I invited my roommate along. We had a great time and got to know each other in a relaxed environment without the stresses of classes, moving in, and everything else that goes on during the first weeks of school.

By the time we had arrived at school, we already knew each other, each other's personalities and boundaries, and what to expect, so things went smoothly and we avoided conflict easily. A great way to avoid conflict is to establish boundaries immediately. This applies to a roommate who may be a stranger to you, like mine was, as well as to a close friend whom you may be rooming with: boundaries can provide a solid foundation upon which to build a new relationship and a means by which to preserve an established one. Make it a priority to schedule a few minutes to sit down with your roommate and discuss each other's boundaries, recognizing the ones you share and working to compromise on those that you don't. But be sure to respect all of them.

Remember, too, that things may come up throughout the school year that may make those boundaries shift. If your roommate knows that you like to go to bed early and he or she wants to pull an all-nighter halfway through the school year, that's something that the two of you need to address. The conversation about boundaries shouldn't begin and end with that initial discussion; it should be an ongoing conversation. Make sure you stay in communication with each other.

Get in touch with your future classmates. The other new freshmen at your school are the only people who are in the same, unique situation you are in and who are experiencing the same gamut of emotions associated with this major transition. Making connections before you reach campus can make the transition easier. Join Facebook groups, twitter feeds, message boards, and any other type of social media that will allow you to connect with and get to know other students in your class.

Specifically, try to focus your attention on social groups whose members are students with whom you will be interacting on a daily basis. For example, I joined Facebook groups that were created for my dorm, my orientation group, and my freshman seminar. Everyone in the dorm group posted our room numbers and who our roommates were. We also exchanged information about how the dorm was set up, room dimensions, and any other information that anyone came across and wanted to share. It was a great way to connect with neighbors before ever arriving on campus, and being able to recognize faces immediately upon arriving gave me a sense of familiarity and security.

COLLEGE LEARNING

ACADEMICS

Declare early, but not too early. Avoid declaring your major in your first semester, and, if you can help it, in your first year. It is so important to take advantage of the wide variety of courses available to you and to use your first year to test the waters of each subject in which you are even mildly interested. Even if you think you know what you want to major in, give yourself some time to make new discoveries and take new courses. I entered Dickinson sure that I was going to major in Sociology; but after taking several courses in writing, one of my true passions, I changed my mind and decided to major in English and minor in creative writing. So give yourself permission to explore.

> **Even if you think you know what you want to major in, give yourself some time to make new discoveries and take new courses; but once you have decided what you want to major in, be ready to declare quickly.**

Once you have decided what you want to major in, be ready to declare quickly. Declaring quickly may give you first priority in course selection within a major and will give you more time to meet any major and/or graduation course requirements. Mapping out your requirements, and what courses will satisfy them, is very helpful. Also, be sure that you have thoroughly researched all the graduation requirements so that you can select courses within your major that meet both major and graduation requirements. Remain in touch with your academic adviser, who is a great resource and who can answer any questions about courses and requirements.

Make connections. Having attended a liberal arts college, I have become a huge proponent of a liberal arts education. One of the key skills with which my own liberal arts education supplied me is the ability to draw connections between seemingly unrelated topics. I remember recognizing parallels between my religion, English, sociology and even geology courses, and being amazed at how much overlap there really is in all aspects of life and study, if you are only willing to see it.

Drawing connections between your French class and your history class, for example, will allow you to apply the French material to a new, historical context outside of the linguistic context in which you originally learned it. This will supply you with a much more multidimensional understanding of both the French material and the history material; and thus, you will get a better grasp on both subjects. Honing this unique skill will not only allow you to think more creatively, universally, and critically throughout your college career, but will also prepare you to continue doing so in the "real world" and in future careers. Fostering this ability will prove to be a benefit in any field or industry.

STUDYING ABROAD AND THE COLLEGE EXPERIENCE

If you are interested in studying abroad, I highly recommend that you seize that opportunity. I studied abroad for a full academic year at the University of East Anglia in Norwich, England, and it was an invaluable and formative experience that I will never forget.

Studying abroad supplies you with the ability to look at situations, experiences, and physical places from new perspectives. Above all, studying abroad supplied me with the ability to look at my own college experience from a different, more critical and discerning, perspective.

> **Studying abroad supplies you with the ability to look at situations, experiences, and physical places from new perspectives. It is an experience unlike any other.**

My freshman seminar at Dickinson was called "Mediated Realities," which examined how the media, the political arena, and institutions are mediated, or manipulated, to achieve an agenda. We decided that a college or university is a mediated reality, in a way. A college or university, like any institution, has an agenda, and that is to impart knowledge to its students; and the reality of the college experience, then, is mediated in order to achieve this agenda.

The college experience is mediated in many ways, one of which is a physical mediation: it's like Disney World. It is a place that stands alone, that exists almost in a bubble: a student could spend all four years at a school without setting foot outside the campus. Because the campus is isolated, in a way, from the rest of the world, it tends to take on its own set of values, characteristics, and idiosyncrasies, however subtle; and these all work cooperatively to mediate the experience within that college or university. Studying abroad prevents that isolation and, therefore, that mediation. You will be exposed to new value systems and cultural characteristics, and then bring that knowledge back to your own campus; and that is a beautiful thing.

The study abroad experience provides you with both a geographical and emotional distance that shatters the illusion, that allows you to see what is being mediated, and how. It allows you to step outside yourself, outside your own world and the "world" of your institution, and look at your college experience from an objective vantage point. It is an experience unlike any other. Aside from that, it is a lot of fun!

TAKE ADVANTAGE

Take advantage of any and all services and opportunities that your school offers that are helpful to you. You, your parents or guardians, the state and federal government, or any combination of these are paying a lot for tuition, books and supplies, and other fees to create the best college experience possible for you. Put that money to work by creating that experience for yourself. Use the fitness center, pool, tennis courts, climbing wall, dance studio, and track. Go to movie screenings, attend lectures and performances, peruse the library archive collections, visit the art galleries, and go to dances. Participate in class, reach out to and engage your professors during office hours, and read those very expensive textbooks. You only get one chance to do undergrad. Do it right, and milk it for all it's worth. It may easily be the only time in your life in which you have so much available to you right at your fingertips.

COLLEGE LIFE

THE FIRST FEW WEEKS

Breathe. Inhale. Exhale. Repeat.

Get involved. One of my favorite quotations is from *The Departed*, in which Jack Nicholson's character, Frank Costello, says, "I don't want to be a product of my environment; I want my environment to be a product of me." This can be true for you in your college environment. Get involved, engage, interact, and make *your* college environment, and college experience, a product of yourself.

There will be ample opportunities to get involved, especially in the first few weeks when almost every club and organization on campus will be recruiting freshmen. If something sounds even mildly interesting, try it! The worst that could happen is that you are miserable at it and the entire club laughs you right out of there. And even then, I promise, you'll survive and eventually find your niche.

When you do find that niche, however, don't close yourself off to other opportunities outside it.

THE FIRST FEW WEEKS

- Get involved, engage, interact, and make your college environment, and college experience, a product of yourself.
- If something sounds even mildly interesting, try it.
- Find your niche.
- Don't close yourself off to opportunities outside of your niche.
- Gets lots of sleep and drink lots of water.
- Establish boundaries with your roommate.

People so often fall into a routine, fall into a group of friends, and become stagnant and thereby forfeit any opportunity to grow and evolve and have new experiences. So, don't be afraid to try new things not only during your freshman year, but throughout your entire college career, as well.

Get lots of sleep and drink lots of water. As clichéd as it sounds, it is so true. The first few weeks, and especially orientation, will require a lot of energy as you rush from activity to seminar, to lecture, to the cafeteria and then the dorm, to the bookstore, and back to more activities. . . . Eventually, you will want to drop. This period of time can be extremely physically, emotionally, and mentally exhausting as you are getting settled and learning the ropes.

Stay hydrated if you are involved in orientation activities and try to get lots of rest to prepare for long days, because you don't want to wear yourself out before the semester is fully under way. You will have four years to party till dawn if that's your thing; but in the first month, take care of yourself and give your mind and body the time it needs to make the transition.

PARTYING

Regardless of whether you are attending Brigham Young University or the University of Texas, students are going to party. You don't have to participate, but know that drinking and underage drinking are realities on college campuses across the country. My intention in raising this issue is neither to oppose nor defend college "party culture" but to urge you to make your own decisions carefully.

If you choose to participate in the "party scene," avoid going out alone and use the buddy system when going out in groups. Be sure to look out for your friends and don't be afraid to interfere if you notice someone trying to take advantage of a friend or peer. Likewise, if you think you yourself have had too much to drink, remember that you have a personal responsibility to check yourself and ensure that you are being respectful of others.

If you choose not to participate in the party scene, know that there are many substance-free events on college campuses such as movie screenings, dances, and comedy shows in which you can participate as an alternative to partygoing. Check weekly or monthly bulletins to stay informed about what activities your school is offering. Many schools also offer substance-free housing, which is a great option for students who are hoping to avoid the party scene altogether.

Regardless of the decisions we may make, all any of us really wants is to have fun. The best way to ensure that everyone is having a good time is to respect everyone and their decisions. Failing to respect a peer could have consequences as trivial as a ruined night out or as grave as a sexual assault conviction. Showing each other respect is the best way to guarantee that everyone will be safe and have fun!

HOUSING

I lived in several different types of housing: a dorm, a flat, and off-campus housing. I spent my first year in a traditional double, with a roommate of my same gender, in a coed dorm. My floor was coed and was split into a boys' and girls' wing, each with its own bathroom. I shared a bathroom (which had four toilet stalls and two shower stalls) with about twenty-five other girls. I remember mornings being particularly crazy, so, ladies, I would recommend getting up early to shower if you can muster up the energy, or waiting until the afternoon when things quiet down. Also, bring a pair of shower shoes! I picked up a cheap pair at a dollar store that lasted me three years.

My second year was spent in an on-campus flat while I was studying abroad in England. I had my own bedroom and a *very* small bathroom called a "pod" (you could sit on the toilet and wash one hand in the sink and the other in the shower all at the same time), and shared a kitchen with seven other flatmates. Even though I got along very well with my roommate the previous year, I loved having the independence and privacy that came with having my own room. I also enjoyed the independence of cooking my own meals and budgeting my biweekly stipend in order to do my own food shopping rather than rely on a cafeteria. It offered me a sense of responsibility and a taste of the "real world" that I probably wouldn't have experienced had I not studied abroad.

If you are planning on studying abroad, research what kind of housing options are available and make sure you are comfortable with those living arrangements. At Dickinson, some programs housed students in on-campus flats, others in off-campus flats, and others with host families. So if you would feel uncomfortable living with a host family, for example, then those programs that only offer host family placement may not be right for you. Just know your own limitations and plan accordingly.

During my final year at Dickinson, I lived in an off-campus house with two roommates. After living pretty much on my own in England, I couldn't see myself moving back into a dorm, and I thought that off-campus housing would offer me the independence that I had gotten used to while abroad. It did. I loved having my own house and my own space. Especially while writing my thesis, it was really important to me to be able to compartmentalize and separate my school life and my home life. I was so glad that I was able to leave the work and stress of school on campus and go home to relax.

Living off-campus, however, did also come with much more responsibility. When you live on campus, everything is taken care of for you: landscaping, maintenance, cooking, cleaning, security—everything. When you live off-campus, you will likely have to take care of most of those things yourself, and then some. You are also responsible for things like signing legal documents with your landlord, shoveling snow (if it snows where you live), paying rent and utility bills on time, being aware of any parking restrictions on your street, and abiding by any neighborhood or community standards or town regulations. It's a lot more work, but it may be worth it for someone who is looking for a more independent college experience and can handle the added responsibility.

TAKE TIME FOR YOURSELF

As a college student, your primary identity is just that: a college student. During college, I allowed my identity as a college student to eclipse my other identities—writer, artist, friend—so that studying and doing schoolwork became most important to me. Looking back, that is one of my biggest regrets. I pushed myself so hard that I missed out on a lot of experiences that would have been really fun, if I had remembered to take more time for myself and the other things in my life that were important to me.

Remember to always recognize, and not to neglect, *all* the aspects of your identity, especially those outside of that of a student. If you're a dancer, dance when you're feeling stressed. If you're a singer, sing. If you're an athlete, play a pickup game whenever you have a half hour free. I put the other aspects of myself on the back burner to focus on school, and I wish I hadn't. I urge you to remember all the things you love and to be sure to make time for them. It will help you reduce stress and, most importantly, stay true to who you are.

> I pushed myself so hard that I missed out on a lot of experiences that would have been really fun if I had remembered to take more time for myself and the other things in my life that were important to me.

STAYING TRUE TO WHO YOU ARE

Staying true to yourself in college can be difficult. The college environment is one that is inundated with a lot of ideas and opinions—many times forceful or opposing ones. You have the college Democrats on (appropriately) the left hand and the college Republicans on the right. You may be involved in a protest that you feel passionately about, as I was, and read hurtful, or even hateful, messages in response to the protest.

Remain open to new ideas and be willing to have your opinions challenged; but keep in mind, too, that you aren't going to agree with, or like, everyone at your school or their opinions, and not everyone is going agree with, or like, you and your opinions, and that's okay. Maintain the relationships that are healthy for you and let the rest roll off your back. Surrounding yourself with healthy relationships is one of the best ways to ensure that you are staying true to yourself and is one of the most important ways to take time for yourself, as well.

> **Remain open to new ideas and be willing to have your opinions challenged, but keep in mind that you aren't going to agree with, or like, everyone at your school, and not everyone is going to agree with, or like, you. And that's okay.**

LOOKING FORWARD

Life goes on, I promise. I'm living proof. While you are in school, you will feel a lot of pressure to perform. You may feel as if writing that research paper that's due next week is an insurmountable task, one that carries a tremendous amount of weight. I know how difficult it can be to see past the next due date or the next exam. But the reality is that in a couple of years, or maybe even in a couple of months, you won't even remember the grade you received on that paper.

You may not be able to see past next week, let alone past graduation; but the "real world" is out there, and it's big. So don't sweat the small stuff, because even though that grade may not seem like "small stuff" now, it someday will be, because your school, your life, the world, everything is bigger than you think it is.

AND MOST IMPORTANTLY . . .

- You know yourself better than anyone else does. You know where your own passions lie, what does and doesn't interest you, and where your limitations lie. So follow your heart and your gut.

- Don't worry about looking stupid or failing. Those are inevitable. Just relax and have fun while you are doing it.

- Don't choose a major based on how much money you think you can make in that field. There is a book titled *Do What You Love, the Money Will Follow.* Try to take that into consideration.

- Show others the same kindness and respect that you show yourself. And if you don't know how to show yourself kindness and respect, find someone who can teach you.

- Don't be afraid.

- And the final, best piece of advice I can give you, and implore you to carry with you beyond college and throughout the rest of your life, is this:

  Illegitimis non carborundum. ★

For more from Anya go to
www.nowyoutellmebooks.com/college.

KELLY FLEMING

"It could've been worse."

A mathematics and statistic major, Kelly used statistics (of course) to help him make the decision to attend Columbia University in New York City. Figures like "10 percent of the student body is involved in Greek life" (he wasn't big on Greek) and "1.5 percent of freshmen transfer after their first year" (he wanted to go somewhere the students really liked) played into the equation. Yet none of the numbers prepared him for what college life was really like. It was this catch-all phrase that got him through the toughest challenges he faced: *it could've been worse.*

MISTAKES I WASN'T PREPARED TO MAKE

I made several big mistakes in college. One in particular I made during my sophomore year, on a night when the subway in New York was running late . . . again. A group of friends and I were on our way downtown to dance off the stress of pending term-paper deadlines and finals, and at two o'clock in the morning, I was running on two Red Bulls and a bag of M&Ms. I sat on the edge of the platform and looked down the long dark tunnel, hoping to see the light from an approaching train, but no luck. Moments like those are what I miss most about college.

I felt a tap on my shoulder. I stood up and brought my cross-eyed gaze to the face of a man in jeans and a T-shirt. He told me I couldn't sit at the edge of the platform; it was dangerous. I told him I understood and I wouldn't do it again. Then he asked me for my ID. Who was this guy? He took out a badge. I went three shades paler. I took out my wallet and the officer interrupted, "What's that?" He was pointing to the first ID I flipped to . . . a fake one. *Stupid*. I turned to the officer, shrugged, and said, "Uh . . . it's not mine." He took it and asked me for my real one. I flipped through the cards and stumbled upon another ID. It was my older brother's expired license. *SO stupid!* A few months later, I left a courthouse in downtown Manhattan having paid a two-hundred-dollar fine for disorderly conduct. Two years after that, I shook the hand of President Lee Bollinger of Columbia University in front of thousands of onlookers and accepted a bachelor's degree with a major in mathematics and statistics.

> "What's that?" He was pointing to the first ID I flipped to . . . a fake one. Stupid. I turned to the officer and shrugged, "Uh . . . it's not mine."

It could've been worse.

A baseball scout is trying to decide between two players to fill a spot on his baseball team. Both players run to first base and arrive at the same time.

Player A gets there with perfect form, but Player B gets there with terrible form. Which player does the scout pick? The answer is Player B because he has more room for improvement. Making mistakes reminds me that wherever I am now in life is only a fraction of my full potential. If I never made any mistakes, how could I ever learn from them and improve myself? All of the mistakes I made in college set me back a bit, but none of them truly prevented me from accomplishing my most important goals: graduating with a degree and loving my four years at college.

COLLEGE LEARNING

HOW TO PREPARE

At this point, I'll assume you've already decided where you want to go to college based more on location, cost, and culture than its name, since your two top priorities should be earning a degree and learning more about yourself. After all, the name of your school isn't nearly as important as the degree itself and how positive and productive your college experience is. So at this point, there are three things you should do to prepare before moving in: network, inform, and pack.

Network. Use tools like Facebook and Google+ to interact with other people going to your school. Get in touch with your roommate to coordinate packing. If your roommate is already bringing a TV, refrigerator, and Xbox, you might have room in the car for your unopened karaoke machine featuring hits from the fifties and sixties (yes, I did that freshman year). Plus, having some name recognition on Facebook before going to school could work as an excellent (or potentially awkward, but fun anyway) icebreaker one day.

Inform. Warning: the first few weeks of freshman year fly by fast! Take some time before move-in to look into everything offered at your school.

Look up meal plans, sports, clubs, service opportunities, academic pro-grams, student life policies, and anything else you can think of. Make a list of any clubs or organizations you think you'd like to get involved in. Then, when you get there, you will be prepared to send out e-mails and Facebook messages to those groups to get more information. And, perhaps most importantly, study a map of the campus! I was late to five of the ten first classes I had freshman year, which wouldn't have happened if I had memorized a map or had been born with a sense of direction. Also, it's a lot safer to know your way around campus, especially if it's located in an urban setting like Columbia.

Pack. Packing is always a hassle, but if you do it right from the start, you can save tons of time and money. Here are a few tips to supplement the obvious:

- Bathroom materials. Bring a shower caddy to avoid clutter with your roommates' toiletries. Bring flip-flops for the shower and bathroom; things can get disgusting, so it's best to be prepared. If you don't have a floor-wide bathroom, you might also want to bring a plunger.

- Laptop. It doesn't have to be fancy. You just need a fast and conve-nient way to access the Internet and use software. And don't buy any of those RPG video games; they will suck the life out of you. If you're having trouble affording your own laptop, try contacting your school's financial services department or the alumni office as colleges are increasingly finding ways to loan them to their students.

- Refrigerator. Even if you never cook, you really need to have one of these to store cold drinks and the leftover General Tso's chicken you ordered yesterday. You can almost always get one on campus from a former student for fifty to a hundred bucks, and it will save you money on food by providing storage for leftovers. As for me, I enjoyed sticking my head in the freezer compartment on hot, humid days in Manhattan. But it's okay because the refrigerator was Energy Star certified, so I didn't cause global warming.

- Taboo or Apples-to-Apples. Maybe it was just my group of friends at Columbia, but we all loved us a good, competitive game of Taboo or Apples-to-Apples. If the trend has changed and the hip games are different, I understand, but it's still a good idea to bring some sort of simple but fun group activity to do with your friends.

- Decorations. Posters, rugs, lamps, pictures, Irish flags, wisdom teeth . . . whatever you do, do something. Better to be weird than dull. Just make sure your room has some personality, even if it says absolutely nothing about you.

WHEN YOU SET FOOT ON CAMPUS, START OUT ON THE RIGHT FOOT

So now you've finished your first great summer as a high school graduate and have officially moved into your college dorm room. You've taken only about a third of my advice and immediately regret having brought that stripper dance pole to be the centerpiece of your room. But that doesn't matter now, because all you need to worry about at this point is devising a plan. Too many people spend all their time deciding which college to go to and forget to figure out how they plan to optimize *living* through college. Once you're there, your focus should revolve around earning a degree while living a good life. To do that, you'll need to define what you want to accomplish and plan how you'll

KELLY'S FAVORITE ONLINE RESOURCES

- Wolframalpha.com
- LeechBlock
- RescueTime
- evernote.com
- reddit.com
- dropbox.com
- 1saleaday.com
- nycgo.com/restaurantweek
- futureme.org

For a more comprehensive list, visit nowyoutellmebooks.com/college.

work on reaching those goals. My college experience revolved around three main goals: earning a college degree, making connections, and creating memorable experiences.

EARNING YOUR DEGREE

Academically, college is a lot different than high school. Rather than being just another kid required by law to go to school every day, you're a college-accepted adult seeking an educational experience that will elevate you to the status of an elite academic scholar. Or you're there so your parents will cover your living expenses for four more years. Either way, you are at class by personal choice each and every time you go. That means that college professors won't treat you like a kid, and all of your effort will be matched by your professors'. That means that if you ask a dumb question because you weren't paying attention, your professor will make a joke about your eighties-style haircut. If you did your homework and ask a good question, your professor and teaching assistants will work hard to help you, though you won't get a star sticker for good behavior anymore. But if you don't put effort in, you won't get any help in return.

When it comes to classes, your priorities should be simple: do your home-work, go to class, and go to office hours if you need extra help. In addition to the basics, here are a few simple tips on how to do well in class without stressing out:

- Meet your classmates. At each and every class, you will have two good, guaranteed opportunities to meet new people: before class starts and after class ends. Try to meet a different person each day. You almost always choose where you sit, and you generally have five or so minutes before the class starts to have a short conversation. If you get a conversation started before class, you have a clear, ice-broken path to a follow-up chat, number exchange, and potential new friend (or hook-up for the scandalous).

- Recap what you learned or studied each day to your parents. You don't have to teach them, but explaining what you learned to someone who has no clue what you're talking about but chooses to listen to you anyway is a great way to save a lot of time on studying. Plus, your parents will be happy that you're talking to them, and you won't have to tell them about your late-night escapades because you'll have something else to talk about.

- Use the Internet. Just about anything you study in college will have study guides and extra tools available online. Most of my professors posted lecture notes, examples, and solutions online, and many of my textbooks had online solutions manuals. Bookmark useful websites like Wolframalpha.com, which is a great tool for remembering how to do complicated calculations, and organize your classes and online resources to maximize productivity. If time-wasting sites like Facebook or twitter are too tempting during study hours, use tools like LeechBlock and RescueTime to prevent yourself from slacking.

The years that you spend earning your degree may be the last you ever spend in a classroom, so do your best to make it the best experience possible. My senior year, I took The Sociology of Sexuality, and from day one, I was the absolute minority in a lecture hall filled with intelligent, inquisitive, and passionate students: of about one hundred students, I was the only guy. After being born and raised with two brothers and no sisters and spending four years at an all-boys Catholic high school, I was in unfamiliar territory. And we were studying the development of sexual stereotypes and heteronormativity in the West. And my name is Kelly, which, as many have often pointed out throughout my life, is a girl's name. But that class was possibly one of the most interesting classes I took in college, and I swear I did not date or try to date any of my classmates. It's amazing how much you can learn when you put yourself in an uncomfortable, challenging position.

And if the discomfort ever becomes too stressful, just relax and remember: *it could be worse.*

COLLEGE LIFE

MAKING CONNECTIONS

Connecting with new people. When you put yourself in the uncomfortable situation of talking to a new person, try to make yourself as comfortable as possible. I met a number of my best college friends in my first semester by simply wearing a New England Patriots jersey and eating chips and queso while watching football in the lounge on Sundays. Find the things that you are comfortable doing, and then do them in uncomfortable social environments where you can meet new people or get to know current friends better.

> Of the many people you'll meet and forget about in college, you will never forget who you lived with, so try extra hard to make the relationship a positive one.

Connecting with your roommate. There are two things you should do to help make the roommate experience much more bearable. First, get out of your room. Being cooped up in a room with someone else for too long can get annoying. Spend more of your time elsewhere, such as in a library, coffee shop, or park. Second, get out of the room with your roommate. Most roommate fights are instigated by the simple fact that the roommates are stressed out and trapped inside their rooms. If you get out and go somewhere together, it'll cheer you both up and you'll end up having an easier time dealing with the chores that roommates often fight over, like doing dishes, cleaning, or taking out the trash. Of the many people you'll meet and forget about in college, you will never forget who you lived with, so try extra hard to make the relationship a positive one.

Connecting and networking. Personally, I'd do better with less Facebook, but everyone should network a bit. Add friends and keep in touch on social networking sites. Go to parties and social events hosted by student groups and keep yourself well informed of potential networking opportunities around campus. Try new things, swap contact information with the people you meet, and be willing to approach new people, even the seemingly unapproachable ones.

Tim Ferris gave lectures at Princeton University encouraging his students to get in contact with hard-to-reach people. A number of his students returned to class weeks later with e-mails and phone messages they had received from movie celebrities, Fortune 100 CEOs, and military generals. Most people are unwilling to have the uncomfortable yet necessary conversations it takes to build relationships with such people, and so there's really not much competition. So, although people often say, "It's not what you know, it's who know," it's also true that anyone can get to know anyone, as long as you're willing to put yourself out there and network.

The dating connection. Without a doubt, dating is the most pleasurable distraction in college. But after classes, dating is just one of the many other aspects of the rest of your life, so make sure it doesn't consume you. If you want to date, find someone who not only makes you feel good about yourself, but also gets you to work harder, be more adventurous, and act with greater integrity. Some dating tips:

- Obtain consent and use protection.

- Gain trust and independence. Both partners must trust one another to keep promises, commitments, and secrets, yet both must still maintain their own independent lives and respect that of their partner. These are the two most important factors in developing a positive, mutually productive relationship in college.

- Sex is overrated, risky, and never necessary. Of course it's fun, but don't let social pressures push you to make bad sexual decisions. Everyone talks about it, but no one is better for having more of it, so don't make your decisions based on what those around you may think. Be responsible and safe.

One of my saddest days came early sophomore year. Thus far, college dating was something I abused and earned unwarranted pleasure from. There were several points in the past year when I had found myself in more than one open relationship at the same time, and though I wasn't cheating by definition, I was certainly in the immature profession of heart-breaking. But one Sunday morning at my parent's house (off campus), my sins came back to haunt me. Waking up in gym shorts and a T-shirt, I opened my eyes and gradually focused on the figures of three women I had affections for. Never before had I seen all three at the same time, but there they were, all standing before me, having conspired to confront (and possibly destroy) me. That day, three long relationships ended forever. Four hearts were broken, including mine. Though I escaped with my life and health, I hit an all-time low. My grades plummeted that semester as I let thoughts of regret and self-loathing expend my time and energy.

Eventually I was able to return to the dating game and improve my academic performance after coming to the conclusion that *it could've been worse, but I can do better.* Never think it'll get easier, because it usually just gets harder as more challenges come. The dating game is tough, but it's also potentially rewarding, so don't close yourself off from new experiences because of the risks. Keep your chin up and your eyes downfield.

CREATING MEMORABLE EXPERIENCES

If you graduate with a degree and have made good, long-lasting connections, you've probably had a decent college experience. But what are you going to remember when you look back years from now? What memories and experiences will you cherish, and which ones will help to shape the successful and happy adult you will one day become? There's a plethora of cool and interesting things you can explore in college. All you need is to know how to find the activities that interest you and have the courage to pursue them.

Travel. Explore as often as you can while you're young and in college, because it only gets harder to find the time later. Finances permitting, take a few long weekends off by leaving campus and exploring someplace new. Go visit another friend at a different school, or go away with your college friends. Go camping; go on a road trip. If you can find the money, visit another country over one of your breaks. I remember spring breaks in Mexico, camping in the Adirondacks, traveling through Europe on a student budget (which meant staying in hostels), and road trips to Canada and Florida. Save up from a part-time or summer job for travel rather than spending it all on cars and clothes. The experiences will be worth it, and the memories will last longer than your shiny new rims.

> Save up from a part-time or summer job for travel rather than spending it all on cars and clothes. The experiences will be worth it, and the memories will last longer than your shiny new rims.

Take risks. Don't do anything illegal or stupid, but have the courage to challenge yourself. If you don't agree with what the professor is saying, speak up and argue your point. If you have an interesting idea for a paper but aren't sure if your professor will like it, write it anyway. If you have a crush on a classmate, ask him or her out. If a friend asks you to go on a road trip to a music festival with him or her, try to find the time. Go for it. Part of the college experience is learning not just about Plato and Aristotle but about yourself. Learn about your own strengths and weaknesses and interact with new people every day. Taking risks can open you up to enlightening and memorable new experiences.

NO MAJOR REGRETS

At one point or another, you may begin to think that you may have chosen the wrong school or the wrong major. You can't distract yourself in life with thoughts of regret. Everyone has them, but you can choose not to get put down by them.

Your major is not all that important. What I really mean is that it's not all that crucial to deciding where you want your career and life to go. It is important that you choose a major that will engage you in classes you find interesting, even if you don't think those classes will help your career down the road. For my major electives, I didn't specifically choose classes that covered potential financial formulas I should know if I wanted to be an analyst. I took Quantum Mechanics and Cryptography, neither of which I expect to ever use again. But I enjoyed the classes and loved what I learned from them. Broaden your horizons and explore your interest while you can, rather than focusing on what's to come tomorrow.

Ten years from now, what you studied in college will be almost entirely unrelated to what you do on a daily and weekly basis. As an intern at New York Life Insurance Company last summer, most of my supervisors were earning six-figure salaries. Only one went to an Ivy League school, about half went to state or city colleges, and most did not major in finance, business, math, or statistics. But they all loved their jobs, made good money doing them, and had these two additional things in common: they all had at least a bachelor's degree, and they all had interesting stories to tell from their college years. So when it comes to major or career decisions, don't regret your decisions and don't let other people shape what you think is important. Your career down the road should be built to suit you, not the other way around.

SUMMING IT ALL UP

Bill Gates never graduated from college. Neither did Henry Ford, Rachael Ray, John D. Rockefeller, or Steven Spielberg. I just graduated from one of the top academic undergraduate colleges in the world, and I am quite sure I will never be on the same lists as Gates, Ford, or Rockefeller. But that doesn't dampen my spirits, because I don't let other people's vision of success affect my own. For me, success doesn't mean billions of dollars or fame. Success is about making every year of my life worth living, whether I'm making a million dollars a year or just a few thousand. And life is about love, memories, and living with integrity. I can accomplish those things equally well as a plumber, teacher, or Fortune 500 CEO.

In the end, it doesn't matter where you chose to go to school, what your major was, who you dated in college, or what jobs or internships you had. You just need to be content with the path your life embarks on, because oftentimes you really can't control it. Life is a roller coaster you don't ever have to get back in line for, so why get off? Take the peaks with the plunges and simply enjoy the ride. ★

For more from Kelly go to
www.nowyoutellmebooks.com/college.

IMANI FINN

"Learn about yourself. Learn about the world."

When Imani arrived at Howard University, a historically black university in Washington, D.C., her world was turned upside down. But despite graduating from a rural, predominantly white high school, Imani quickly settled in to life at Howard. She is currently a junior and majoring in clinical laboratory science.

LIFE AT AN HBCU

I had originally wanted to go to NYU and Howard was my second or third choice. I did get into NYU, but then I got a full ride to Howard, tuition and housing paid, and it kind of made up my mind. I wouldn't recommend this type of decision-making to everyone, and at first I wasn't sure if I had chosen the right school. But now that I'm in my junior year, I can honestly say that it ended up being the best decision I ever made.

Being at an HBCU (historically black college or university) has been a new and mind-blowing thing. It makes me look at the world differently and had forced me out of my comfort zone.

I grew up in a predominantly white town in a rural area, and for the most part I wasn't really friends with the few kids that were black. So throughout my whole life, a majority of my friends were white. And don't get me wrong, I loved my friends: black, white, green, or otherwise, they were still my friends. The way we clicked went beyond skin color, and the friendships I'm still making today are not based on what color you are or where you're from. But being at an HBCU (historically black college or university) allows me to be around a majority of people who look like me, which is a new and mind-blowing thing. It makes me look at the world differently and has forced me out of my comfort zone. I love it.

At Howard, 90 percent of the people are my color, and these are people from all different walks of life, who want to learn, *and* they look like me! To see this many educated black people every day gives me hope for the future and has changed my view of the world.

COLLEGE LEARNING

PROFESSORS 101

Every instructor has some part of his or her teaching style or some habit that will irk you. Even if you work well with them and click with them, even if they are one of your closest mentors, there will always be *something*. Some are unreasonably hard graders. Some don't care about extenuating circumstances. Some don't teach the way you expect them to. Most act like their class is the only one you're taking. I have had teachers who do all of the above. And you deal with it. You just have to. Because at the end of the day, you are there to learn, and if they make you work a little bit harder for that A, then so be it.

If they don't care about extenuating circumstances, then you may have to get a dean or someone else with more authority involved, because if you are extremely sick or something else is going on that's an emergency, then a professor should really give you a break and you need to find someone to help you make that happen.

I had one professor freshman year who I still believe is the most . . . let's say "not nice" teacher ever. I ended the class with a B average, but the grade was lowered because she had a super-strict attendance policy. If you missed more than two classes, she'd started to deduct points, which is understandable. Over the whole semester, I missed four classes and two of those I missed because I was sick with strep, which was documented with a doctor's note. But when grades came, I had a D, and I had to repeat the course. To this day, I don't understand the math she used to justify giving me an unfair grade that was two full letter grades lower than the grade I had earned. Unfair teachers are the most difficult.

Even though I had some difficult professors, I never really had a *dreadful* one thanks to ratemyprofessor.com. It's a *wonderful* tool and everyone should use it if at all possible. But even for the ones I didn't mesh well with, I just had to find ways to work around it. That's life. You can't always avoid situations just because they aren't ideal.

MAKING DECISIONS, MAKING MISTAKES

College is the time to make mistakes. For me, college has been one of the most indecisive times of my entire life, so I was bound to make some. Coming into school, I knew I wanted to be a doctor. I have wanted to be one since I was five years old. But I didn't know which major I wanted to study. A million thoughts ran through my mind: "Do I pick a science major? Do I want to do political science so that I can go to law school *and* medical school and practice medical malpractice law? Do I become a chemical engineer so I still have a lucrative career to fall back on if I decide not to go to med school?" And even though I've declared a major now, I still have questions about what I want to do after school: "Should I go to medical school? Should I be a dentist, or maybe an optometrist? Which tests do I need to take? Which path is more conducive to having a family? Is all of the time I'd spend in medical school and residency worth it to *me*?" So really, once you declare a major, it just opens up different doors and provides new and different questions. The questions and the decision-making process never end.

> It can sometimes be hard to pick one path and stick to it, but that's part of what college is about: learning to make decisions and learning from your mistakes.

You will make mistakes and have to make decisions as you figure out what path you want to take. It can sometimes be hard to pick one path and stick to it, but that's part of what college is about: learning to make decisions and learning from your mistakes.

REGRETS, I'VE HAD A FEW

On the one hand, the college experience is more than just an academic education, but on the other, academics are really the reason why you're there in the first place. I forgot that, first semester of freshman year, and I started to skip classes. I may have gone one or two times a week per class. I didn't do my assignments like I should have, I didn't really study too much, and if I did, I waited until the night before to do it. I was one of the biggest slackers ever. It was horrible. At the end of that first semester, I had a 2.94. It wasn't a bad GPA, but it definitely wasn't good, and definitely not the kind of grade that I was used to in high school. But it was exactly the grade I deserved.

Looking back, I realize that I just got so caught up in having freedom from my parents and being able to set my own rules that I temporarily forgot I was there to get an education. More than anything in my life and my college career, this is what I regret, because I know that I am so much better than that. But my temporary lapse in judgment motivates me even more now, so it was a lesson that I needed to learn, and I'm glad that I did.

COLLEGE LIFE

FINDING YOUR WAY

One thing I didn't expect when I got to school was that most of my friends from home didn't stay my friends. It's not something that a lot of people will tell you about college. I think I was too idealistic about that; I thought my friends and I would all stay close. But that's life. You have to kind of find your way on your own. So my first year, I tried to meet new people everywhere: in the advisers' office trying to figure out who my adviser actually was; in the ridiculous line for financial aid; in my first class at 8:10 a.m., when I found out they'd switched my professor at the last minute. You can meet new people in the clubs you want to join, or in the cafeteria on a day when you have to go by yourself. Just be open to meeting all different types of people, and that will lead to finding someone you truly click with and who will be a lasting friend to you.

Also, be sure to explore your surrounding area. For me, going to school in Washington, D.C., has its perks because there is always something to do, or at least something to explore in the area. No matter where you go to school, you aren't there to just learn about your major; you're also there to learn about different people and different environments. You're there to learn how to interact with people you like and people you don't like, to learn how to live without your parents in an unfamiliar area, and to learn how to become familiar with that area. It's all part of the college experience. When your parents come to visit, you should be able to help them find their way around your campus. And if you can't, something is seriously wrong!

The same goes for academics. College is so much more than just an academic education, and if you just spend your four years hitting the books, you'll miss out on the fun you could have had, the people you could have met, the nights you would have never forgotten, and the love you could have found. College is about learning about yourself, learning about the world. You just can't do that if you're holed up on campus.

HOMECOMING

The life of a college student is different at an HBCU. Homecoming becomes the biggest event of the year, and we're not talking about the football game. At most predominantly white schools (what we at Howard call PWIs, or predominantly white institutions), if Homecoming is a big deal on their campus, it's usually about the parade, the game, and maybe a dance or party. But on HBCU campuses, Homecoming is a weeklong event. At Howard we have different events every night like a gospel concert, comedy show, celebrity basketball game, poetry reading, fashion show, and step show.

TOP FOUR SURVIVAL SKILLS

The main things that will help you maintain your sanity (somewhat) during your college years are naps, time management, eating a healthy, balanced diet, and finding time to unwind and relax.

Naps are one of the most cherished things in any college kid's life. They give you just a few hours of calm away from the craziness. If you have to pull an all-nighter (and you *will* probably have to pull an all-nighter at least once, no matter how organized you are), a nap helps refresh your mind so when you wake up you can really focus on the task at hand. It's like a pushing a reset button for your brain, which is important because there is so much material that you are taking in.

Finding time to relax is crucial to mental survival in college. You need to be able to find time in your schedule to not be a student or an employee or whatever other role you play. You need time to just be you and spend time doing things for yourself, whether it's just watching TV or taking a stroll or crocheting, like I do. Whatever you need to do to relax, find time to do it so you don't go crazy.

One thing I think every college student should *make* time for is dating. To me, dating is essential to your growth. You don't necessarily have to be in a relationship, just go on dates! You will get to know so many different types of people, get to know the types you like and don't like, and that will make it easier to see when someone is truly compatible with you when they do come along.

Time management is really the most important thing because it allows you to have the time to do everything else. How else would you have the time to shop for healthy groceries, go on a date or get a good night's sleep when you have to worry about the test you forgot about or the project you didn't complete? Keeping up with everything can be hard. Sometimes you want to fall off the bandwagon and not go to class, or not do your work or whatever. But keep in mind that you're paying for your education, so you should do your best to try to get the most out of it, and that means scheduling the time for it. I try to stay on top of things with a daily planner, a dry erase calendar and the iCal on my Mac. All of them sync up to help me keep track of what I need to do and when, and it tends to work pretty well for me.

LIFE SKILLS

Even though you're at college to get an education, the life skills you gain while in college are more important than a degree. You learn how to network with people and make connections, how to write professional e-mails, how to manage your time, and how to manage your freedom. College is really just a microcosm of the real world.

College is such an exciting time, and you will have so many different opportunities thrown at you, that it's sometimes hard to remember that you aren't there just to get involved and get an education, but also to learn about the world and more importantly, learn about yourself.

College is a microcosm of the real world.

When you are a teenager in high school, you tend to go through a period where you think you know yourself so well: you think that how you act at that age is how you will always operate. But really at that point you have no idea. Meeting new people and being away from home for the first time will more than likely either completely change how you look at things or solidify the views you already have. Either way, it will affect who you are and how you interact with your surroundings.

One extreme I've seen is when people let hobbies and the things they are involved in shape them, and I don't want that to be me. I don't want to join a group and not know myself enough that I allow the others in that group to put me in a mold. I will only disappoint myself in the long run. Pretty much, if you want to change or reinvent yourself, then cool. But don't let anyone ever change you just to make you fit in. Knowing who you are is really a skill that college will teach you, and changing who you are should only ever be your decision.

Ultimately, you need to make your college experience your own. It's good to have input from other people who have gone through it, but honestly, it's an experience you need to create for yourself. It's something that you will never forget. ★

For more from Imani go to
www.nowyoutellmebooks.com/college.

THOMAS GRONEMAN

"College is as hardcore as you want it to be."

Though Tom's decision to attend film school in Los Angeles had something to do with Robert De Niro's performance in *Goodfellas*, his decision to make the best of his college experience was entirely his own. He learned, sometimes the hard way, the dos and don'ts of college life. Like: don't bring your autographed picture of Darth Vader to the dorm, and do eat your veggies; don't grow a beard, and do realize that though the college years are great, your best years are yet to come.

COLLEGE LEARNING

CHOOSING A SCHOOL

Choosing a college is such a scary proposition. For years, your parents and teachers make the college decision into the be-all-end-all decision of your life. It *is* a huge decision, but it doesn't hold sway over the next fifty years. When you graduate you're only twenty-one freakin' years old! You have at least nine more years to get it together before your life is over!

I applied to a lot of film and liberal arts schools (NYU, UCLA, UC Berkeley, Hofstra, Emerson, and Boston College) once I figured out that the only true skill I had developed or had interest in developing in high school was storytelling. I chose Loyola Marymount University because it is located in Los Angeles, had an amazing campus, and, well, I just wanted to get as far away as possible from my hometown. I wanted to try to make it on my own.

Sometimes I wish I had chosen an alternate career or a school in a different section of the country. In fact, I was depressed for a long time and I regretted the choices I had made. But one day you realize that no matter what path you choose, you'll always wonder what life would have been like down an alternate course. If you truly love what you're doing and enjoy the friendships you've made, then great! If not, you can always start again down a different road.

I have grown in more ways than I think I fully realize, and when I think back to when I was eighteen and fresh off the plane, I can see now how naive and inexperienced I was. But I'm glad I stuck with film school and stuck with LMU, even though I had my doubts. I'm glad I did my growing in L.A.

CHOOSING A MAJOR

I always loved writing. I wrote poetry and short stories all the time in middle school and high school. (And not crappy, lovey-dovey poetry. My poetry was deep and philosophical, man.) I originally wanted to be a novelist but I don't like how there's no "wrong" answer when interpreting literature. I also didn't have 450 pages of story within me dying to get out.

Fortunately, I love watching and making movies. Then one day, as I was watching the behind-the-scenes of *The Return of the King*, I came to the realization that film was what I wanted to do, and I chose screenwriting because I knew I'd be passionate enough to want to study it for four years. It also might be because 90 percent of what my father said to me as a boy had been previously uttered by Robert De Niro in *Raging Bull* and *Goodfellas,* so I was pretty attuned to movie dialogue from the beginning.

If you're unsure about what major to choose—don't stress. Plenty of people go into college undecided or switch majors a bunch of times. No one is locked into the course of study they initially decide upon, and don't let anyone make you feel like that initial decision will determine everything that follows. It is more important to try to find a school setting and environment that you think you'll enjoy and a solid academic program.

No one is locked into the course of study they initially decide upon, and don't let anyone make you feel like that initial decision will determine everything that follows.

WHAT TO DO YOU BEFORE AND AFTER YOU ARRIVE

- Prepare for homesickness. I brought my favorite pictures of my friends and family, which was supposed to inspire me to do great things. It ended up only making me miss home.

- Do *not* bring your autographed picture of Darth Vader. This will *not*—I repeat, *NOT*—get you laid.

- Once you arrive, get involved in various organizations around campus—service organizations and the like. If I could go back, I would actually take surfing lessons.

- Be outgoing.

> **Remember that every other incoming freshman is in the same boat as you. They are all nervous, they are all unsure of themselves, and they all think the RA is hot.**

- Remember that every other incoming freshman is in the same boat as you. They are all nervous, they are all unsure of themselves, and they all think the RA is hot.

- Do not buy a black shirt that says "College" on it. John Belushi drank himself to death and you're not nearly as funny as Jim Belushi, let alone John.

- Don't grow a beard.

- Talk to everyone you can. Talk to every guy, talk to every girl. You will never again make more friends in any given two-week span than you will during the first two weeks of your college transition. Everyone needs friends and everyone will be interested in you . . . at least at first. Here are some helpful questions to ask during those early conversations:

  Hi, I'm _____. What's your name?
  What's your major?
  Where are you from?
  What kind of music do you listen to?
  Do you want to see my room?
  Why don't you want to see my room?!
  Where are you going?!?!
  OH *GOD*, WHY AM I SO ALONE?!?!?!

PROFESSORS 101

The hardest thing to do in college is to care about a class you aren't interested in. I like to emulate the actions and philosophies of the Mahatma when faced with a dreadful professor: passive-aggressive resistance and nonviolent protest. I surf the Web, I don't take notes, I argue with my fellow students in class, and I fall asleep. Take *that*, Survey of Mass Media!

Every professor who teaches within a film school is in some way jaded, pretentious, or sometimes a downright career failure. They constantly form their comments about your work based on their own preferences and background rather than encouraging your own creativity. There are exceptions, of course, but the best way to handle it is to find friends who are egoless and free of pretension and joke about it during class.

I like to emulate the actions and philosophies of the Mahatma when faced with a dreadful professor: passive-aggressive resistance and nonviolent protest.

Do as my younger brother does, and gently lean your face forward into the palm of your hands and sigh deeply every thirty seconds or so until your six-hour cinematography class gets out or your buddy sets fire to his own jeans. Personally, I find a friend in class and make sure to exchange pained and horrified looks that escalate depending on the level of pretension or bullsh-- that spews like a Geyser of Ignorance from your classmates' or professor's mouth.

TRYING TO SAY ON TRACK

Everyone eventually falls behind with his or her work. *Everyone*. No matter what promises or oaths you swear silently in the night to whatever gods you worship about staying on top of your game and kickin' ass in every class—it doesn't always happen. College is as much a social experience as it is academic. If high school is a Siberian gulag, college is the prison camp from *The Great Escape*. It's as hardcore as you want it to be.

You quickly learn that success in the college environment is all about choice. "Will I *choose* to stay in and write a paper about Immanuel Kant's underwear drawer or will I *choose* to adorn my body in school memorabilia and streak around the quad drunkenly with my buddies?" When you get home after four hours of class, a full shift at work, and an unexpected two-hour e-board meeting and then realize you haven't eaten anything that day—the answer to the previous question becomes clear. It's time to break out the body paint.

What you *can* do to help yourself stay on track is get enough sleep (at least five hours, HA!) every night, and make time for three square meals. Seriously, with enough sleep and enough food, I can handle anything the world throws at me. Therefore, so can you.

COLLEGE LIFE

THE ROOMMATE RELATIONSHIP

Believe it or not, it's pretty easy to end up with a good roommate freshman year. In fact, the administration engineers things that way through various orientation groups and questionnaires about rooming preferences.

More than likely, your relationship with your roommate will progress through each of the following four stages:

Genesis. The awkward first phone call before moving in. The meeting of the parents, who are always either (a) overly protective or (b) very angry. The first conversation about Pokémon (wait three to five days before initiating). A beautiful friendship, perhaps built out of necessity, begins.

Unification. Construction of the FFC, or the Freshmen Friendship Corps, of which your roommate will, by default, be a member. Make the most of your time with these friends during freshman year, because they will start dropping like flies early sophomore year. Possible commonalities among FFC friends: you have the same or a similar major; you both have siblings; neither of you has a car; you share political views; you both like turtles.

Bromance. You've been through heaven and hell with your roommate. You are seen so much around campus together people think you're a couple—a Pax Bromana, if you will.

Schism. Your roommate gets a girlfriend or boyfriend. Worst-case scenario: they've never had a girlfriend or boyfriend before. They spend *way* too much time together, they invade your personal space, and they fool around on your futon Tuesday night before your 8 a.m. Wednesday class. They bicker and argue around you, and slowly but surely you are replaced—all because they don't know how to manage time well. "What do you mean you can't watch *Mystery Science Theater 3000* tonight!? *NO*, YOU CAN'T INVITE YOUR GIRLFRIEND!!!"

The Schism is tragic and unavoidable. Just bide your time and wait for things between them to slowly self-destruct. They will.

DATING

I'm attracted to girls who make me nervous. Oh, and girls who look me in the eye. And talk to me. I guess I'm attracted to you, too, if you never talk to me. I don't have a type but I am drawn to girls who are outgoing, confident, and easy to talk to. Intellectuals with the ability to make me laugh or keep me guessing. Someone who breaks through my pessimistic, sarcastic exterior and speaks to the real romantic underneath. Jesus, what is this, a match.com profile? My favorite food is "milksteak."

I've never been a womanizer and depending on your own circumstances, it may be really easy or really difficult to find someone at college who is worth your time. One thing I would definitely not recommend is starting a long-distance relationship or entering college while in one. Everyone should meet and date new people with different views and talents. What better place to do that than in college? So the best thing to do is to attend a wide range of social events that attract different demographics. I mean, I DON'T KNOW! Try holding the door open for a lady once in a while, you animals!

There's plenty of time for romance, don't worry. Just try to balance your time and make sure things don't get too serious too early. Oh, and eventually you have to come to terms with the fact that you're not going to find lasting romance drunk in someone's yard off-campus.

WORK

One thing that I learned is that it's really, really hard to save up money if you're not working full-time. But you should still get a job. On campus or off. Get two jobs. Start supporting yourself early. Also, take on more and more responsibility as the years go by. Prove to yourself that you can progress personally and professionally, and start building that resumé because, man . . . graduation is approaching and I'm pretty frightened. I mean, I'm prepared but . . . oh God. . . .

MAKING HEALTHY CHOICES (OR TRYING TO, ANYWAY)

Step one. Don't join a frat or sorority.

Step two. Move off-campus. Buy vegetables. Cook vegetables. Because if you stay on campus, you'll step into the school cafeteria one day and realize it's been three and a half months since you've tasted something greenish. Green beer doesn't count.

Step three. If you can't move off-campus, go home frequently, and tell your mother how much you love her before and after every home-cooked meal.

Step four. Buy a pull-up bar.

Step five. "What's that? There's a gym on campus? I'll be there every day! Hell yes, I'm going to improve my body *and* my mind!" Repeat this phrase as necessary at the beginning of every semester until graduation, or else this will happen:

Average Gym Visits per Year:

Freshman: 72

Sophomore: 48

Junior: 7

Senior: FIFTY-CENT TACOS AT JACK IN THE BOX?!?!?!

THINGS TO AVOID

Avoid joining a frat if you can. I have never been a frat guy but I don't think paying dues to an organization to prove that you're a "cool" guy sounds like the reason you worked your ass off in high school. Many people join these groups to "cut loose." Trust me, you can cut loose pretty hard without spending a thousand dollars a year on dues. There are great things frats and sororities do—they raise money and awareness and put on some pretty awesome events—but if you choose a major like filmmaking, where your life is based on working on projects outside of class all the time, Greek life can be a distraction.

Also, don't smoke. I started smoking and just recently quit. The urge never truly leaves you and that is a scary notion. I haven't smoked for three months but as soon as I catch a whiff of someone else lighting up—it's all I think about. L.A. hates smokers. People smoke pot, eat 'shrooms, and score coke, but apparently, *smoking* is frowned upon. I miss New York.

Other than that, avoid "Sailor Jerry's." I would also recommend Kraken Spiced Rum only in moderation.

GREAT EXPECTATIONS

One expectation that no one should have coming into college is that the "real world" is this big, scary place that materializes after you graduate. As soon as you stop playing with Legos and start taking care of yourself, you're in the real world. And guess what? College is part of it.

The only expectations I have are about the future. Success is all about moving forward. As a writer and filmmaker, I can only hope to have projects to consistently work on and a network of friends and peers I will want to work with creatively in the future. The most amazing scenario would involve selling a feature film script in the next couple of years, but I would be happy if I have a good day job and could focus on writing during my spare time. Staying hungry for new and compelling projects is key in Los Angeles, and my field is one that requires way more independence and personal drive than it takes to simply sit in class and take tests.

Believe it or not, you're not going to make all your important life decisions during college. Do not expect to meet your future wife or husband and to finish maturing fully as an adult. Rather, you have been given your first taste of freedom and you have to treat it responsibly. For some they are the best years of their life, but for most, those years are yet to come. ★

For more from Thomas go to
www.nowyoutellmebooks.com/college.

MALLORY CRAIG

"College will be an adventure. Spread your wings!"

Mallory, a sorority sister and college football fanatic, studied English and education at the University of Arkansas in Fayetteville, just thirty miles away from her home town. There, she developed her three keys to academic success—GET UP; SHOW UP; KEEP UP—and built a fun and thriving social life. Mallory is currently working toward her master of education degree with a certificate to teach English at the secondary level.

COLLEGE LEARNING

CHOOSING A SCHOOL

My connection to the University of Arkansas goes back for generations, and I got generations of advice about attending here. My mom and dad went here; my sisters and brother and their spouses all graduated from U of A. In the beginning I wondered if I should have gone away to school, chosen a school that was a farther distance from home. I wanted a new "adventure." All of my high school friends were enrolling at U of A, which was great, but I felt like I wouldn't have the opportunity to experience anything fresh or new.

Of course, it all worked out. College life at the U of A *has* been an adventure for me; it's inevitable in the college environment, with a campus of 21,000 students, that you will encounter new people, and new ideas, and new experiences. I'm so happy I came to the University of Arkansas.

CHOOSING A MAJOR

My mother is a teacher. My grandmothers were teachers. My great-grandfather was a teacher and a college professor. So my parents urged me to go into education. They said that they really wanted me to get an education degree. (Actually, it was much more forceful than that.)

I had wanted to get an art degree at first. But I was persuaded by my family's advice. They reasoned that a person who goes to college should come out with a practical skill. The country is in an economic recession. But the world will always need teachers; there will always be kids in school in need of an education.

That's why I decided to go into English education. I love to read, and to analyze literature. I have had wonderful English teachers, too, both in high school and college. They inspired me. I want to open up the world of literature for other students like they did for me.

So I got into English, with my eye on a master's in education, and I haven't looked back. It's been a great experience.

BIG LECTURE HALLS

If you choose to attend a big state university, like I did, you are going to end up in some huge classes. They won't all be that way, but some of your general requirements may be lecture classes in which you are one of a sea of students.

If you choose to attend a big state university, like I did, you are going to end up in some huge classes.

When that happens, you have to realize that this is college; it's not the same as high school, where all your teachers knew you and cared about you. This teacher will probably never even know your name. When your teachers don't know you, they won't care about your individual grade. You can't blame them; if the teacher has five hundred students every semester, he or she can't have an intimate relationship with each one.

Since the professor is not going to initiate a teacher-student relationship, you'll have to be sure that you are on top of your assignments, your test dates, and your understanding of the material. Which brings me to my next piece of valuable advice: raise your hand in class!

RAISE YOUR HAND

Don't be afraid to raise your hand. This gives the professor the opportunity to know who you are; and when the instructors know you, it's so much easier to talk to them. You'll be more confident meeting with them to discuss issues about grades or assignments, or a topic you didn't fully understand from the lecture, if you've made an effort to connect with them in class. And as a general rule, professors tend to favor students who participate in class in a positive way.

SECRETS TO ACADEMIC SUCCESS

Here's my motto: GET UP. SHOW UP. KEEP UP. It's true. Following those three practices will bring you academic success.

First, you've got to get up. Get out of bed, even though no one is making you do it. Next, once you are out of bed, you have to show up. You actually have to get dressed and go to class. And once you're in class, you need to keep up. You have to listen to the professor. Pay attention. If you aren't listening, going to class won't help you.

You're paying for these classes; the reason you are here, in college, is to get an education. To accomplish that, you have to follow my three-step plan.

TAKING NOTES

Work hard at taking really good notes. I try to write down everything the professor says—just take it all down, verbatim. Fortunately, I'm a *really* fast writer.

Seriously, taking notes is vital. You'd be surprised how often you can look around a class and see people who don't even attempt it, who don't even have a pen in hand or a sheet of paper in front of them. Of course, assigned readings are important, too; but as a rule of thumb, the things a teacher takes the time to talk about in class are going to be the areas of greatest importance. Be sure to take good notes, and review them before the exam.

SCHEDULING

Make yourself attend class. You'll always know what to anticipate, and what's around the corner, if you are present and listening. Keeping a planner helps. And when it comes time to register, here's some advice: never take four classes on a Tuesday/Thursday schedule.

PROFESSORS 101

Most of my classes in college have been great, but you have to understand that you'll like some classes more than others. And you'll enjoy some teachers a lot, others not so much.

I've had some dinosaurs. One professor of mine had been at the university since the Second World War. The 1940s, anyway. I'm not kidding. Now, that's quite a career, and it's admirable in many ways. But it's clear that, by this time, his teaching style is set in stone. You are not going to change him. And if there is anything that you wish was different in the way he runs his class, forget it.

So, stick it out. You have to adapt to his way of doing things. There's a lot to learn from someone who has been around that long. Look on it as an exercise for the real world.

On the other hand, I've also had the privilege of taking tremendous classes with wonderful professors at U of A. One of my favorites was an English professor who taught Modern American Literature and African American Literature. He demanded a lot of us, requiring us to read twelve novels in each course. But he had such a way of engaging his classes: he made you want to do the reading; you wanted him to be impressed by your paper.

He assigned one book that was controversial to some because it related to our community, but that made it so relevant to our experience. It was eye-opening. He taught us to see the history and continued existence of social struggles that I'd never been taught before. When a teacher makes you see the world in a different way, that's one of the rewards of the college experience.

When a teacher makes you see the world in a different way, that's one of the rewards of the college experience.

PREPARING FOR AN EXAM

Here's a tip: never, ever go out the night before a test. I only did it once, the night before a geology test, but it's a really bad idea. It will bring you bad luck, I promise. It's like bad karma, you know?

If you stay in like you should, studying your notes and text and getting to bed on time, you'll be rested and ready to go on exam day. You'll have on your game face. And you'll be able to write, to think, to nail down answers.

This probably seems like a no-brainer, but just wait till temptation strikes. Resist it!

COLLEGE LIFE

ROOMMATES

With roommates you have to have respect for each another, and sustain that day to day. Whether you choose a roommate or are assigned one, there's a possibility that you will not have anything in common. On the other hand, you may end up being great friends. Either way, you have to accept that person and create a good environment so that you can live together successfully.

You should know that you won't necessarily meet your group of new best friends on the first day of college. Just sit back and let the chips fall into place, because they will. I didn't even know that some of my best friends existed in the first semester of my freshman year, but over time I have encountered the most amazing people. Joining a sorority gave me a leg up on making new friendships. But there are lots of places where you'll find friends in college: organizations, dorms, and classes. One of my best friends is a girl I happened to sit by in Drawing I. We got to know each other in class, and now we're inseparable.

MALLORY'S MOTTO

- GET UP. Get out of bed, you lazy head!
- SHOW UP. Get to class. Attendance is key.
- KEEP UP. Take excellent notes and stay on top of your work.

FOOTBALL CULTURE

Being a fan of University of Arkansas football is a fact of life on this campus. At Arkansas, football is king. I think that's generally true on southern university campuses. It may have something to do with the fact that, in the South, there aren't as many professional sports teams, so the fans really rally for the college teams. And in Arkansas the whole state really revolves around the U of A teams.

This focus on college athletics is wonderful. There's such a heartbeat to it. It makes people have so much pride in the school. It transcends the game; it's like a symbol of the state of Arkansas that we all gather to support. There is a sense of camaraderie in the fans. When you come to Arkansas, our pride in the sports teams is contagious.

You have to witness a big game day to really understand it. There are tailgate parties a mile long, with people eating and laughing and getting fired up. Folks set up their tailgate tents at 8:00 a.m. for a 5:00 p.m. game because you have to: there's such a crowd, so much excitement. If you want to book a hotel room in Fayetteville, you have to get it long before the football season starts. On game day the students get all dressed up; guys in suits and girls in cocktail dresses. Those suits can get pretty hot in August, but it's a tradition in the fraternities. There are glitter banners on all the fraternity and sorority houses; even the buildings get dressed up. Win or lose, game day is fantastic. Of course, at Arkansas there's lots more winning than losing.

SOCIAL LIFE IN A SORORITY

I joined a sorority when I came to U of A, and I'd strongly recommend rushing to anyone. The Fayetteville campus is big, as I said, with a really large student population, and that can be overwhelming unless you can find a group to be a part of. Also, when you're from a nearby town and you come to such a huge campus, there's a danger that you'll cling to your two or three high school friends and never branch out to meet anyone new.

A sorority is a way to network and make new friends. It takes that big campus and gives you a focused group to belong to.

The sorority I joined fixed that situation. A sorority is a way to network and make new friends. It takes that big campus and gives you a focused group to belong to. It provides an identifying connection.

My pledge class had eighty-five people; that's a lot of girls, all kinds of personalities. The sorority also requires that the pledges take part in lots of activities, and that keeps you busy and involved: a sure antidote to boredom or loneliness.

The Greek organizations also encourage academic excellence. My sorority has the highest GPA on campus, and it requires that the pledges make their grades before they can be initiated. The sorority has a study hall that the pledges have to go to; and they introduce you to the library, which is something everyone in college benefits from. The fact that the older girls in my sorority put this emphasis on academics had a very positive influence on me. When a peer, someone you admire, tells you that you have to make your grades, it makes you want to excel.

SELF-AWARENESS

In college you get to know yourself. You can find out who you really are, what you think, what you believe.

When I was in high school, I was with the same group of people that I'd known for twelve years. That's good in a lot of ways; it provides you with a secure foundation, but it can be hard to get past the stereotypes. People pigeonhole you in seventh grade, and it follows you for the rest of your life. That stunts you in high school.

> **People who don't listen in college don't change. People who just swallow it all may change too much.**

In college you break through those limitations. You are exposed to new people and ideas, and you are not locked into a preset identity or mind-set.

Attending public school in a small town in the Bible Belt, I received a very conservative education. When I got to college, the liberal thought and academic freedom opened up so many new ideas and attitudes. I didn't adopt them all without thinking, but it gave me a chance to filter new ideas. To think about exciting possibilities.

People who don't listen in college don't change. People who just swallow it all may change too much. You must filter all the things you learn and see and hear: filter it so that you can develop your own moral compass.

AND MOST IMPORTANTLY . . .

College is an adventure. Spread your wings! ★

For more from Mallory go to
www.nowyoutellmebooks.com/college.

JOSHUA TANIS

"Don't let anyone stand in the way of what you want to accomplish."

A biology and music double major at SUNY Albany, Josh has earned his reputation as an accomplished student pianist throughout New York's capital region. He plans to attend dental school upon graduation and pursue a graduate degree in music. Josh is the Music Director of the UAlbany Musical Theatre Association and a member of the University Chamber Singers, and, did we mention that he has performed at Carnegie Hall and the Beijing Olympics?

YOU AND YOUR COLLEGE YEARS

You will enjoy a sense of liberty when you are living on your own at college, and that liberty teaches you a lot. You have to learn very quickly how to budget your time and meet deadlines. College, unlike high school, is a place where students are not coddled, and the first few weeks can be rough as you try and figure your way around campus and make sure that your homework and reading assignments are done. But you will soon get a handle on it and fall into a routine. You must learn how to take care of yourself and to adjust to new situations. Mom and Dad aren't going to be there to help you get through the hard times—and yes, there will be hard times.

Despite the fact that going to college comes with great responsibility, it is a time to have fun and take that next step toward becoming an independent adult. There will be many great things that happen during your college career as well as some not-so-great things, but take one day at a time, plan ahead, and look with positivity into the future that college is leading you toward.

COLLEGE LEARNING

CHOOSING A SCHOOL

In my senior year of high school, I applied to and was accepted at three colleges. Once I had ruled out Pittsburgh, the choice was between Wagner College and SUNY Albany. My first impression of SUNY Albany was that it was ugly—an enormous concrete complex. On the other hand, the campus and setting of Wagner College was beautiful. It's set on top of a hill near the Verrazano Bridge and is only a ferry ride away from Manhattan. Being able to commute in and out of the city was a feature that was important to me.

I made my final decision when my mom and dad sat down with me and said that they would cover the expense of my undergraduate education if I went to SUNY Albany. Despite my deep desire to attend Wagner College, I was not looking forward to having to take out student loans to pay $52,000 a year, when the cost at SUNY Albany was only $20,000. (I say *only* as a means of comparison to Wagner.) At the end of our conversation, I decided to enroll at Albany.

Sometimes I do wonder if I chose the right school, but when I look back at my decision, I can't complain. Sure, the campus is hideous and the winters here are long and cold, but I do believe that everything happens for a reason. For example, I have found great success in my music career here in Albany, and I don't think I would have had the same kind of success at Wagner since it is so close to Manhattan, where there are a million pianists fighting for only a couple hundred jobs.

> **That's what college is all about: learning how to make good choices, and learning how to deal with the choices you make.**

My decision to attend SUNY Albany has taught me to find the good in the things that seem, at least at first, far from ideal. That's what college is all about: learning how to make good choices, and learning how to deal positively with the choices you make. Try not to let yourself become overwhelmed by negative thoughts when things don't work out ideally for you. Make the best of what you have and where you are. If you put in the effort, you can succeed in whatever community or school you find yourself.

HAVING A PLAN

I chose to major in biology and music before I even began college. Do I recommend heading off to college having already decided on your major(s)? I'm not sure it works for everyone, but I can't say anything negative about going into college with a plan. It has worked well for me thus far.

I have known from an early age that I was interested in studying music in school. I've been playing the piano for over seventeen years now, and music isn't something that I will ever willingly give up. I knew music would be my major since I knew what college was!

I am also studying biology, and that decision was similarly apparent. With both of my parents being physicians, there was a push for me to study some kind of science in school. Biology is something that I have always enjoyed. Learning about the body and how and why it works is fascinating. I spent a lot of time in high school reading my biology textbooks and pretending like I knew what my parents were talking about when they had discussions in their "doctors' jargon." Biology seemed an obvious choice, and studying biology gives me the opportunity to pursue a career in the health-care industry in the future, whether it's becoming a dentist or a neurophysiologist. The decision to choose both majors was surprisingly clear as I focused on what I wanted to do with my life and what would make me happy in both the present and the future.

CHOOSING CLASSES

Choosing classes is difficult, especially when you have to select them before you know a lot about them, since the registration process usually happens several weeks before the start of the following semester. My advice is to find people who have taken the class previously and ask them about it. Find out what the professor is like, find out how heavy the workload is and how time-consuming the course will be. Knowing a bit about the course that you want to enroll in is crucial, otherwise you may have the stress of having to drop and switch classes at the beginning of the semester.

GETTING TO KNOW YOUR PROFESSORS

One of the most beneficial things you can do at the beginning of each semester is attend your professors' office hours and get to know them. This will be especially helpful when you score a lower grade on an exam than you had hoped. I've found that when professors know you and know that you are a conscientious student, they're more willing to work with you than a student they have never seen before.

Another benefit of getting to know your professors is that you'll have the opportunity to ask them to write you a letter of recommendation for jobs or graduate schools. Receiving a good, personal letter of recommendation from a professor who knows you well will go further than a multitude of good grades.

WHEN A PROFESSOR KNOWS YOU *TOO* WELL . . .

If you do develop a good relationship with your professors, you might find that they have a tendency to look at you during their lectures and direct a lot of their questions at you. This can turn into an uncomfortable situation because the other students understandably stare at you and wonder who you are and why the professor keeps calling on you. I know that professors mean well and just want to reciprocate the interest I have shown, but sitting in a large lecture hall full of four or five hundred people and being singled out can be slightly intimidating and embarrassing.

When that happened, I would just smile and nod or answer the question and play it cool, but it takes a lot of courage to speak up or risk answering a question incorrectly in front of five hundred people. I finally realized after this started to become a regular occurrence that I just needed to deal with it and consider myself fortunate that a professor would think of me when there are five hundred people sitting in front of them. Be prepared for that situation, but really, in the long run, it's a good situation to be in!

COLLEGE LIFE

DIFFERENCES BETWEEN COLLEGE AND HIGH SCHOOL

Looking back, living at home through the end of my high school career was extremely convenient. Having Mom or Dad cook and clean for you is a lot easier than fending for yourself. In college, on days when you aren't feeling well, you'll find yourself doing everything it takes to get your body out of bed and make your way to class, when you may have simply stayed home in high school. Waiting for the bathroom is another inconvenience. Just think of having to stand around in your towel as you wait fifteen, twenty, or even thirty minutes just to get a shower, and then trying to awkwardly shower when you know there are seven other guys showering only inches away from you. Does that happen in high school? Not likely!

College isn't like high school socially, either. When you arrive at college, it's a new start. Your high school career is behind you. Your reputation there, whether good or bad, means nothing to the people you will meet. They won't know anything about it! At the same time, if you're hoping to avoid the drama you may have experienced in high school, forget it. When people say that the pettiness and cliques end in high school, they're wrong. You will find the same kind of cliques in college, just more of them.

FIND YOUR WAY AROUND

Definitely take time to orient yourself as soon as you get to college. Look around for where your classes will be held and where the library is, and become aware of what's around you. Maybe you'll notice that one dining hall looks better than another, or maybe you'll notice a beautiful courtyard that you'll want to study in when the weather is nice. Spend time exploring and take it all in.

One great resource that many colleges offer is freshman tours of the campus. Yes, these can be tedious and sometimes long, but they really will take you almost everywhere and show you exactly what you need to see. But do some exploring on your own, too. SUNY Albany has a tunnel system under the buildings where most classes are held, and the tour I took didn't show us the tunnel system. But by exploring on my own and talking with other students, I realized that these tunnel systems were a great way of getting from class to class during the winter.

MAKE YOURSELF AT HOME

Create a home space for yourself as much as possible. At the end of the day, you want a comfortable place to return to. Think about what you have in your room at home, what makes you feel good and what gives you a sense of comfort. Maybe it's having five pillows on your bed or a poster of your favorite athlete on the wall. Whatever it is that makes you feel good, bring that with you.

Being someone who likes to keep my room bright and alive, I always bring a bright floor lamp and a few desk lamps to keep in my room. I find the standard dorm light fixtures tend to be these dark, fluorescent lights that barely fill the room. Going to school in the North means enduring long winter nights. Besides the fact that seasonal affective disorder can set in, I hate waking up in the morning, going to classes all day, and getting out of classes at 4:00 p.m. when the sun is already going down and it is getting dark! Having a bright room helps alleviate the sense of darkness and tiredness, and helps me to focus on what I need to do instead of dozing off, hopping into bed, or turning on the TV. Being comfortable is a key element to doing well in school. Just remember that your dorm room will be your second home for eight months out of the year.

ROOMMATES

It is nearly impossible not to have at least a minor roommate issue. I unfortunately experienced slightly bigger problems during my sophomore year. My sophomore year roommate was a biology major, too, and we agreed to room together when we were finishing up our freshman year. The first semester went very smoothly and we barely argued about anything. Then, in the second semester, my roommate decided to pledge a fraternity, which led to a number of issues.

Oftentimes I would come back from class and find a stranger sleeping in my roommate's bed, or *my* bed, with the door to the suite and bedroom left wide open. This was a serious issue for me, realizing that strangers had the keys to my room and suite and were invading my space. Almost every night (well, technically morning) at around 3:00 a.m. my roommate and his pledge brothers would come back to the room from their pledging events and would be as noisy and disrespectful as possible: doors would slam, every light would be turned on, and they would sit in our common room and talk loudly while everyone else was trying to sleep.

After trying (and failing) to communicate with my roommate about how his pledging process was affecting us, my suitemates and I tried to take matters into our own hands. If any of the pledge brothers left something in our common room, we would immediately throw it out. If some of them were napping during the day, we would purposely drop heavy books on the floor, slam doors, or even set off air horns in the room! Clearly, some sort of meaningful, but legal, payback was what we were looking for!

After some time, their pledging process finally ended and everything seemed to calm down. Looking back, I should have contacted a Residential Life staff member. If any roommate issues become too out of hand for you to be able to handle on your own, contact your RA or RD and do something about it. You should be able to live peacefully with your college roommates and together create an academic and social environment that works for all of you.

LEARN TO PRIORITIZE

Be innovative. Try new things and offer your talents to your university community. Each one of us has many things that we can bring to our respective colleges, and to let your talents sit on a shelf and collect dust is one of the worst things you can do. At the same time, avoid biting off more than you can chew. College life, especially at the beginning, is rigorous. Allow yourself some time to settle in and develop a routine. Don't feel compelled to do it all. There's really no need to join nine clubs, run for a student senate position, *and* work a part-time job. That's just too much. Budgeting your time wisely will be the best thing you can do for yourself while you're in college.

If you begin to run your body down by doing too much and perhaps not sleeping enough or eating well, you will get sick. Getting sick and missing class, even for a day or two, can put you miles behind. Classes move incredibly quickly in college and professors make little effort to wait for those who fall behind. Think about how much a college professor manages to fit into sixteen weeks, while only going to class a few days a week, versus what a high school teacher stretches across an entire academic year, while going to class every day of the week. That puts it into perspective, doesn't it?

Don't feel compelled to do it all. There's really no need to join nine clubs, run for a student senate position and work a part-time job. That's just too much. Choose a few things that you enjoy doing and stick to them.

Choose a few things that you enjoy doing and stick to them. Bouncing back and forth between too many things will only show people that you don't truly know what you're interested in. Listen to your body when it's telling you that it's tired or overworked. Take into consideration the fact that although you may enjoy doing a vast number of things now, it will all most likely catch up with you, and sooner rather than later.

THE VALUE OF YOUR EDUCATION

Yes, your undergraduate education can be thought of as one key to the rest of your life, but it's also a time to be serious and look to the future while keeping yourself grounded in the here-and-now. Be thankful for you education and try to assess the value and appreciate the meaning of it. If you don't put in the effort, the most you can expect to get out of college is a good party here and there and some interesting friends. But if you put work into being a good and conscientious student, college can be a life-altering experience.

You will come out of college having had training in not just your field of study, but in life. Living and communicating with strangers teaches you more about life than any college class ever will. The thing that makes college so unique is that you are living on your own and experiencing new things all the time.

Living and communicating with strangers teaches you more about life than any college class ever will.

Take in everything and appreciate everything that happens to you. Learn from your mistakes and grow from them, too. When you fall, get back up, keep moving forward, and don't let anyone stand in the way of what you want to accomplish. College itself is a tremendous resource. Use everything to your benefit as you take the next step into your bright future. ★

For more from Joshua go to
www.nowyoutellmebooks.com/college.

CATHERINE RALEIGH

"It's the beginning of your adult life."

Catherine is a young woman who knows what she wants. When choosing a school, she knew that she was looking for a small, private, Catholic school that was close to home. Catherine ended up at Siena College, where she joined volunteer organizations, studied abroad, and made a life for herself away from home.

COLLEGE LEARNING

CHOOSING A SCHOOL

One thing a lot of students wonder about is whether they chose the right school. When I first decided to go to Siena, I was split fifty-fifty with another school, Providence College. I wanted to be in New England really badly and I wanted to be by the beach, both of which Providence had and Siena didn't. Siena also didn't have some of the clubs and other activities I was interested in. For a while I did debate whether I'd made the right choice and whether I should transfer. But the longer I was there, the more I felt at home. That's the big clue. If you're at a school and you feel less and less like it's right, you should probably consider transferring. On the other hand, college is what you make of it, no matter where you are. I'm convinced that you can make almost any school work for you if you're willing to find what's right with your school and work in that direction.

> I'm convinced that you can make almost any school work for you if you're willing to find what's right with your school and work in that direction.

Also, don't believe everything you read in the guidebooks. If you're at a school that isn't ranked quite as highly (and often rankings are subjective), strive harder to stand out. You might be able to make better grades, which will be your ticket to a good grad school.

CHOOSING A MAJOR

I didn't declare my major until the beginning of sophomore year, but I was pretty sure by the middle of freshman year that I wanted political science. Siena requires you to take courses in different areas, so I took political science classes my freshman year to fulfill the requirements, and I loved them! Even the basic classes about contemporary U.S. politics were really interesting. I find international affairs and foreign policy even more interesting, but those are the higher-level courses. You've got to take the basic classes before you can take those—and I realized that was what I wanted to do. I declared my minor as global studies.

Even though I considered a political science major before I left for college, I entered college undeclared, which I still think is the best thing. Of the people I know who declared a major right off, three quarters of them changed it. Even if you're pretty sure, I think it's better to go undeclared.

For one thing, if you declare a major, you usually start in the tougher classes in that subject. I know a lot of science majors who came to college thinking they'd be able to handle it, but the advanced classes were too hard. If they had taken an entry-level bio class before they declared their majors, they might have known that.

However, once you're sure what major you want, it's a good idea to declare it sooner rather than later. I didn't have to declare till the end of my sophomore year, but you don't get an adviser in your department until you declare. The advisers are the ones who can tell you what to do and what classes to take to get the most out of your major. So I wouldn't wait till the end of sophomore year, but I also wouldn't declare before you arrive, either.

PLAN AHEAD TO GET THE COURSES YOU WANT

A problem everyone seems to have is getting the courses you want and need at times that don't conflict with other things. If I'd known how hard it was going to be, I would have planned out my schedule better and done more research on when classes were offered. And I would have done it all as soon as I knew what my major was going to be. I'm finding now that I'm behind because I didn't realize that certain classes are only offered once a year.

DIFFICULT PROFESSORS

I've had a couple of difficult professors. For me, that often simply means that they can be strict or not very outgoing. In one case, I scored badly on my first paper. So I took it and went in and asked him how I could do better going forward.

I worked so much harder on the next paper. I did exactly what he told me to do. Yet when I got it back, I still didn't do very well. I read it over and had others read it over, and I really felt like I deserved a better grade than he'd given me.

I decided I was going to talk to him about it. My friends said, "What are you doing? You can't question a professor like that!" And it was intimidating. But I decided it was my college education, and I might as well know what I was doing wrong. So I went in. I wasn't disrespectful, demanding a better grade or anything. But I'd done my homework, talked to him about what he wanted in a paper and checked in with my classmates on what they did and the grades they got, so I was able to say, "I did what you asked here, and here, and here, and I don't understand why I'm still not giving you what you want."

> That is one of my favorite things about college—the fact that I get the chance to talk with professors beyond the walls of the classroom.

In this case, he said, "I'm sorry, I must have read it too fast. Let me take another look." He did, and he changed the grade to a higher one. That is one of my favorite things about college—the fact that I get the chance to talk with professors beyond the walls of the classroom. It moves learning past just listening in a classroom setting.

The point is not to accuse your professors of grading incorrectly. But do ask questions and be willing to work with them to do better. It's your education.

GREAT PROFESSORS

I had many professors who always managed to get the class involved instead of merely talking at you and expecting you to take notes. The best ones related their topic to real life and helped you understand how the information was valuable to you in the real world—why knowing that material was actually important to your life.

It's also great that, these days, some professors use PowerPoint and will post the slides online. Then, when you're studying for your finals, you have the entire presentation available to you.

YOUR SCHEDULE

The biggest adjustment for me was learning how to deal with class assignments and deadlines. College isn't like high school where you have the same classes every day. In college, you might have a class twice a week, and even then papers or assignments aren't due every time. Things are much more spread out. Learning to budget your time and hand things in on schedule is a big adjustment!

For example, one professor might give you a paper that isn't due for two weeks—but you can't wait until then to start it, because you will have other assignments that will be coming in at that same time. It's a real juggling act. And it's kind of tough to make yourself work on an assignment that isn't due for a week. But you have to!

The truth is, you get used to budgeting your time after a week or two—or after the first time you pull an all-nighter. Yeah, after that, it comes fast!

My scheduling trick is to do homework as soon as I get back from the gym. I like to go to the gym every day. Everybody goes. Usually the girls work out and the boys play sports. It's good for you and it's a good break from studying. It helps you de-stress. So it becomes routine: work out in the gym, then do class work. I'll get certain amount of work done before dinner, a certain amount of work done after dinner, and if I have extra work, then I know I'm not going to have the time to hang out with friends after that.

KEEP YOUR EYE ON THE PRIZE

Now that I've declared a major, I know what I want to have when I graduate: a good understanding of political science and global studies. I'm also planning to have done multiple internships to gain an understanding of what the field is really like.

Then I want to get into a good grad school. I'm considering either law school or going to grad school for foreign policy. Right now I'm looking at international law as a profession, but I'm not sure yet.

I know a lot of people who leave college thinking they're going to have an amazing job right off the bat, but you've really got to plan and learn and take steps to put yourself in the best possible situation.

COLLEGE LIFE

HOMESICKNESS

If this is your first time living away from home, there's going to be an adjustment period, but everyone handles it differently. I thought I would be a mess for weeks. I cried the entire first day I was there—and then I was fine. On the other hand, my cousin got to college and he was fine; he was perfectly happy at first. But then a week later, he started crying. He cried for a week. Then he was fine, too.

> **Make plans, even simple plans, there at school. When you have something to look forward to, you're not thinking about how much you want to be home.**

Have a plan for when you are homesick. Call someone and talk. I called my mom a lot and she understood. My roommate was the third kid in her family to go away to college, and her parents had told her not to call for the first week so she wouldn't become dependent on calling. Personally, it helped me to call home now and then. I would also talk to my friends. Or walk around campus. They always have activities on campus: on a Friday night you can go and watch a movie or games. I did that a lot and that's how I met some of my good friends. Make plans, even simple plans, there at school. When you have something to look forward to, you're not thinking about how much you want to be home.

My advice to parents is to be a good listening ear, but don't immediately say, "Oh, poor baby, I'm coming right now to take you home!" You've got to let go of your kids and let them get past that wall by themselves. I would even say to the students, don't go home the first weekend. Even if you just sit in your room watching movies by yourself, don't go home the first weekend. This is where you're living now. Get used to it. Lots of kids have trouble at the start, but by the third week or so hardly anyone is still nervous.

Remember, no matter who you are, no matter how excited you are to go away to school, you're going to be homesick. Just know that it's coming, even if you don't think it will. But it will go away! By Christmas break you'll get home and after a few days realize you're really looking forward to getting back to your life at school!

SETTLING IN

Of course, the colleges give you lists of things to bring for your dorm room, but some are more important than others. I had my coffeemaker. And bed risers, which are really important. It's never on the list, but you don't have a lot of room in the dorms, and you need somewhere to store stuff. A bed riser lets you raise the height of your bed so you can store stuff under it. A must, for sure. I had to go buy a rug because I forgot about that.

> **The biggest thing I discovered was that I'd brought way too much stuff. You don't need it and there's not enough room!**

As soon as I found out who my roommate was going to be, she and I decided who was bringing the TV and everything like that. You also need extension cords. The biggest thing I discovered was that I'd brought way too much stuff. You don't need it and there's not enough room!

I put a lot of stuff back in the car. For example, you really only need clothing for one season, because you'll be home to get your winter stuff, or they can send it. You also can buy stuff there. You don't need as much you think.

MAKING HEALTHY CHOICES

You can usually tell the freshmen in the food hall. They're the ones eating whatever they want, and lots of it. Soon enough they'll get over the fact that nobody's telling them what to eat. Then you have to start making healthier choices. I always go for the salad bar. Every day you can always find something that is healthy. You have to, or you'll pack on the pounds and feel like you've been eating junk food.

ROOMMATES

Everybody has a roommate story, and here's mine. The first time I chose a roommate it was because we had something in common—we weren't rampant partyers, and neither of us drank. Back in high school, that felt very defining. However, as both she and I came to discover, the fact that we weren't drinkers was about the only thing we had in common. In all other areas, we were like oil and water. As I began to have more experience living with roommates and apartment-mates, it became clear to me that respecting each other and each other's wants and needs is much more important than having a few personal choices in common.

My advice with roommates is to set boundaries from the beginning. My roommate would have her guy friends in the room till two in the morning—at Siena, you can have boys on the floor until midnight during the week and 2:00 a.m. on weekends. Even though it bothered me, I didn't say anything the first week. I thought it was better to get to know a person before saying something. But the truth is, we never really connected. And since I'd never said anything, it became harder and harder to bring it up.

For a roommate situation to work, you've both got to set boundaries from the very beginning. Talk things out. Compromise. It's just basic respect on both people's part.

The second semester, I moved in with someone else. She was the complete opposite of me in many ways. But somehow we got along great! She has become one of my closest friends. When we were roomies, we didn't hang out on weekends, but we got to know and really like each other. Who'd have thought? So sometimes having a narrow definition of who will make a good roommate can get you in trouble. You've got to think about more than one issue.

In high school, the line was distinctly drawn between the partyers and the non-partyers. In college, things are much more complex. You become friends with a whole range of people. Initially, I only thought, "I want a roommate who won't go out partying every Friday night and leave me alone in the room." But you discover that there are all sorts of people doing all sorts of things on Friday night and you have your choice of what you feel like doing. There's always someone to hang out with, even if you feel like staying in.

It was a nice surprise to find out I could be friends with a wide range of people while not changing who I am. It felt very freeing. Also, if you go out with people who are drinking, it doesn't mean you have to drink. You can make your own choices. It's the beginning of your adult life, and you can make wise decisions but still have fun.

Also, I've heard people say, "Be careful about rooming with your friends, because you'll soon discover that when you live with someone, it's completely different." And it's very true! As an RA, I saw lots of friends move in together only to discover that things that don't bother you when you're hanging out as friends can become very annoying when you're roommates. Bedtimes are a big one: if you get along really well, but your friend goes to bed at 9:30 p.m. and you go to bed at 1:30 a.m. and that means you can't work in the room after she has the lights out, it's going to cause tension.

Another thing that's nice about living on campus is that all your friends are right there. If you want a break from studying, you can find someone to hang with. You don't have to call around to find an available friend and go meet them. They're there already!

SOCIAL NETWORKING

Everyone goes on Facebook. It's usually pretty interesting. Of course people get nosy as soon as anything changes: if a relationship ends and you post it, that's a big thing. But you've got to be careful about what photos you put up. Pictures on Facebook have caused problems in school. I'll go on and see freshmen girls who live in my hallway with beers in their hands. What are they thinking?

> **When posting anything on Facebook, a person should ask themselves if it is something they would be ok with professors and employers seeing. If the answer is no, don't post it.**

When posting anything on Facebook, people should ask themselves if it is something they would be okay with professors and employers seeing. If the answer is no, don't post it. But if you use a little common sense, sites like Facebook can be a lot of fun.

BE A JOINER

The best friends I have on campus I met through clubs and common interests. The club fair was the second week of school, and I joined everything I was interested in. Some of it didn't work out, and that's fine. I ended up staying with the ones I really cared about. I met my closest friends through those things.

Even if you didn't belong to clubs in high school, you should join some in college. There is so much you can get involved in. For example, I joined service clubs that help out the local community and go on trips to build houses with Habitat for Humanity. It's helpful to be involved in clubs that go along with your major, too. For example, I'm in Model United Nations to go along with political science. I love it. It's like real-world experience. It's very helpful. Also, internships, internships, internships! That's how you get professional experience and meet people in the field.

I'd also recommend studying abroad. Living in another culture blows your ideas of what's "normal" culture wide open. You will return with a completely different world view, which will help you for the rest of your life. Studying abroad was by far my most powerful college experience!

DATING

Some people go to school thinking that they're going to find their soul mate, or at least a steady date, immediately. But don't count on it during your freshman year.

Being in a dating relationship calls for a schedule adjustment, especially if you're serious about doing well in your classes. It's different than in high school because you're living with the people who are your friends and whom you're dating. They're right down the hall. It's not always good to be able to see people whenever you want. You've got to balance your time. If you've got two free hours, do you work on your paper, or do you hang out? Fortunately, my boyfriend and I were in some of the same classes, which was nice because we could study together and help each other with those classes.

What was important to me when choosing someone to date was his maturity, his morals, the importance of education to him, respect, and an obvious love for his family. It's easier to see those qualities in college because you can tell who the mature ones are by noticing what they do on their weekends and how they respect people. A person's values become apparent when you're with them all the time.

AND MOST IMPORTANTLY . . .

I believe the most important thing you leave college with is a much more comprehensive understanding of life, along with a completely different world view. You will also have become more mature by the time you finish college. You can look back at the choices you made, and even if you see that those choices might not have been so good, you can still rise up and become more mature as a result. ★

For more from Catherine go to
www.nowyoutellmebooks.com/college.

BENJAMIN PEARCE

"Adapt and overcome."

Ben, lover of all things aquatic, is currently pursuing a degree in marine operations with a minor in naval science at the Maritime College of the State University of New York. An avid diver and swimmer and vice president of the Semper Fidelis Society, Ben dreams of becoming an officer in the United States Marine Corps. His plans and hopes for the future are rooted in a profound commitment to serving others and a deep love for his country.

COLLEGE LEARNING

KNOW WHAT TO BRING AND HOW TO PREPARE

My karate instructor from home always remarked, "Those who fail to prepare, prepare to fail." This is especially true when preparing for life at a military academy or military-lifestyle college. Two of the most important ways you can prepare are by packing wisely and by staying mentally and physically in shape.

Every college has a "what to bring" list that is either posted online, given out during orientation, or mailed home. But the key difference for someone attending a military academy or military-lifestyle college is that this list isn't a suggestion: whether you arrive as a civilian student or report to the Regiment of Cadets, you will be required upon arrival to bring *only* the supplies on the provided list. Showing up with extra belongings can lead to unwanted attention or unwanted hassles during move-in. Only after you go through the indoctrination process will you be allowed to bring a cell phone, computer, clocks, watches, and other "forbidden" items.

It's also important to prepare by staying in shape. A physical fitness regimen is encouraged before arrival at any military college. This will enhance your ability to adapt to the physical demands that will be put on you while at college and will greatly reduce challenges under physical stress.

While it is important to sharpen your body, you need to keep your mind even sharper. Whether you have set out on a journey to eventually lead people within the U.S. military or lead business associates in the corporate world, you have to be able to make difficult decisions with a clear mind. That means knowing when and how to make a decision that could be the final call in a business deal, or even, in a military situation, a decision that determines who lives and who dies. This is pretty serious stuff for an eighteen-year-old who is fresh out of high school! So it is important to stay sharp. The initial training received in the Regimental Indoctrination Program or during college orientation can help promote that kind of ethical and critical thinking.

NETWORKING

Whether your goal is to make friends or establish professional contacts, networking is extremely important. I remember when I first showed up to orientation in the fall, I introduced myself to about ten other kids within my incoming class. This helped me assimilate and get to know my college family, and helped me feel like I had made the right decision to live a regimented lifestyle.

Networking in each of your classes is also important. Get at least two or three contact numbers from each class and share yours. That will allow you to pass around information, communicate with others about the class, and make plans to study together. Be sure to stay after class and introduce yourself to the professor, too, and express your appreciation and excitement about being his or her student. This makes the professor feel respected, leaves a lasting mark upon you, and demonstrates how much you value your academic success.

ROOMMATES

After you learn who your roommate is, don't make premature judgments about how good a roommate you think he or she will be. How they dress or look will be modified by a military haircut and a khaki uniform anyway. Try to maintain a positive attitude and tell yourself that you are really lucky to have him or her as your first roommate. Try to identify any life experiences or hobbies that you share: you may have more in common than you think! And remember that you both have a guaranteed common ground: you've both chosen to become a part of the great tradition of studying at a military college.

ADAPT AND OVERCOME

You may feel a little overwhelmed as an incoming freshman. When you do, just remember that you can adapt to and overcome any difficult changes or challenges you encounter. You will be challenged in ways you never knew existed, but is this as difficult as Navy SEAL training? No way! You can definitely overcome any obstacle when you set your mind to it.

It's also important to realize that there will be upperclassmen and superiors there to pick you up, support you, and help you to correct a poor decision that could result in reprimand or injury. Your superiors and upperclassmen will blaze a trail ahead of you and show you that anything is possible with the right desire and a little planning.

I remember one of the first speeches by my college's president, Vice Admiral John Craine. He remarked, "This is a place where faculty and peers want to see you succeed. You can do anything you want in this world with the support you will receive from myself and my staff. Dreams *do* come true at this school and within this family." This was very moving for me because it spoke to the difficulty of the military lifestyle and provided me with the strength to adapt and overcome with the help of my new community. This was a beacon of hope for a lot of my shipmates, as well: it's an amazing feeling to become part of such a tradition and family.

GET INVOLVED, BUT NOT TOO INVOLVED

It is very important to join extracurricular clubs within a military college. And whether you want to exercise a musical talent, join a drill rifle or saber team, or even try an extreme sport like scuba diving, most military colleges have a lot more to offer than civilian colleges! So don't be afraid to take advantage of what is offered and try new things.

Military colleges are also usually very well known for their athletics, because physical training requirements help support athletic programs probably more than the student athlete realizes. In my case, I got recruited to play lacrosse but decided after playing for one season that it wasn't for me. Then I approached the head coach of the men's swimming team because I wanted to stay in shape. He said, "Jump in the pool and let's see what you've got!" I ended up becoming an NCAA Division III conference rookie the first week of my first season! The bond I developed with the swim team has to be one of the most significant things that has ever happened to me in my life. Point being, you don't know how extracurriculars can impact your life and lead to such wonderful things you never dreamed of.

But getting involved also means that you have to acknowledge your academic responsibility over any other commitments, *including your military obligations*! You should look to the upperclassmen and officers that you admire for the skills that are necessary to multitask and organize: learn by their example.

Never put yourself in a position where you have to choose between con-current activities. If you do find yourself in that position, you must take responsibility, sit down with advisers from both parties, and negotiate how you can divide your time.

If you are feeling overwhelmed and overly involved, you need to take a moment to ask yourself, "Am I getting in over my head?" or "Am I involved in too many activities for

Stress is caused when people feel that others expect a lot of them, and they cannot understand how to satisfy all parties.

my own good?" Answering these questions honestly and assessing which obligations are most important can help reduce stress. Stress is caused when people feel that others expect a lot of them, and they cannot understand how to satisfy all parties. Remember that.

One of my first Marine officers I was counseled by, Second Lieutenant Cano, often exclaimed, "Work hard, play hard!" Make sure you make time to play to reduce stress.

COLLEGE LIFE

MAKING HEALTHY CHOICES

While you attempt to balance your obligations and meet others' expectations of you, it is very important that you never neglect your own personal health and that you maintain a healthy lifestyle. Hydrate often, take power naps (if you are able to set an alarm clock!), and eat healthy. Choose the apple over the brownie and remember that even a small healthy decision goes a long way. If you aren't eating right, malnutrition can lead to susceptibility to colds and viruses. Studies show that stress within a military environment can often be caused by poor diet, which can lead to poor physical and academic performance.

If you have a sore throat that lasts for longer than a couple of days, get it checked out. If you have a bad stomachache, report it to sick bay or the infirmary. You have nothing to be ashamed of when reporting medical concerns or admitting that you may be coming down with something; it doesn't mean you're weak. It's expected that you will see to your health as well as protect your peers and subordinates from contracting any illness that you may be fighting.

RESPONSIBLE PARTYING

Obviously, there is no perfect world where no one drinks in college. Odds are, you aren't twenty-one yet but already drink socially. Underage drinking happens, even at colleges with severe penalties for drinking offenses. Oftentimes, military colleges will exercise a zero tolerance policy, which means that social drinking is banned from school grounds and that offenders will be punished severely. Remember that you are bound to the college's integrity policies from the very first moment you arrive through the front gate, so make sure you have assessed the risks and are being responsible.

You won't be a professional beer pong player ten years after you graduate!

If you do intend to drink, never go out alone and always practice the buddy system. Be cautious of where your drink is located and never let it leave your field of vision. It's not uncommon for others to try to slip something in your drink; I have even witnessed it and stopped it!

Am I trying to talk you out of underage drinking? No, but I am encouraging you to be wary of your surroundings and to not lose sight of your goals. It's not worth sacrificing them for one night of anarchy, and you won't be a professional beer pong player ten years after you graduate! You want to be a person of honor and valor whose character and ethical values are what defines him. Remember that, and if you are going to drink, drink responsibly.

STAYING TRUE TO YOURSELF

The military college environment will set out to strip you of your individualism and generate a team member, because teamwork is the most important aspect of the military. The success of this country's armed forces, economy, and political system is due to each American citizen's ability to work together toward a common goal.

But through all that, it's important to maintain your sense of humor, your personality, and your ability to reach out to others. Take from others only what you like within their personalities and notice the things you don't like or don't appreciate. Learn from others' mistakes and learn from your own, because no one ever learned anything from doing something the right way. Officers, upperclassmen, and your families want to see you succeed, so don't forget to stay true to yourself as you try to satisfy all commitments.

Learn from others' mistakes and learn from your own, because no one ever learned anything from doing something the right way.

AND MOST IMPORTANTLY . . .

A squad leader once said, "The worst truth is better than the best lie." This is true for any aspect of military college life. Knowing what to expect is important because it could affect your decision to succeed or fail. And it is just that: a decision that you must make for yourself. All I can do is tell

You must make the decision whether to succeed or fail, and the power to succeed is ultimately within yourself.

you from my experiences what I think you should know and do to prepare for life in a military college. The power to succeed is ultimately within yourself.

You have networks and support systems available at your military college, and you should identify them and utilize them as much as possible to help you succeed. The eyes of your communities are upon you, waiting for you to do so. I thank you for considering the burden of practicing the tradition within this country's history that is attending a military college. ★

For more from Benjamin go to
www.nowyoutellmebooks.com/college.

"The things that aren't perfect about college are exactly what make the experience valuable."

A fter winning the Foot Locker Cross Country National Championship during her junior year of high school, Aislinn experienced an uncomfortable spotlight, and began looking at big schools where she could blend in with the crowd. She ended up at the University of Colorado at Boulder, where she studied studio art and sculpture. Eventually, Aislinn had to give up her sport and passion, running, but she gained deep friendships, valuable knowledge, and life-changing experiences that she would never forget.

COLLEGE LEARNING

HOW I CHOSE MY SCHOOL

I liked the idea of going to a big school. At the same time, I knew I wanted a campus with gorgeous surroundings and an outdoor oasis nearby. Even though UC Boulder has both those things, I ultimately chose it based on the success of their running program, as that was my focus at the time. I ran in high school and was recruited by a number of colleges, but I trusted the coach at UC Boulder more than any other coach I met. That made the decision a little easier. But when it came time for the final decision, I went with a grid system—a chart with pros and cons, different colored markers and ratings—and much discussion with family and friends.

It's interesting to wonder how my life would have been different if I had chosen another school, but the reason it took me so long to make a decision in the first place was because I knew that I wanted to commit to a school and stick it out. And I did.

STAYING ON TRACK

College is a lot less routine than high school. I love that freedom. In high school, I felt trapped by the repetition and the expectation that things would stay the same way they've always been. In college, it's a whole different story; you are completely in charge of everything about your experience. But with that independence comes added responsibility, and it's up to you to keep on top of things.

One thing that helped me stay motivated was making the school work personal. In other words, do what you have to do to make the assignments mean something to you. I love to learn, so I knew that if I wanted to get the most out of class, I had to put as much time into the readings and assignments as I possibly could. Maybe your motivation is that you don't want to look silly or like you don't know what you're talking about. Maybe you're taking this class as a requirement and you need to do well in order to graduate. Whatever is, find something that will help motivate you.

Another thing that will really help is learning to speed read and type flawlessly. These are two very important skills for college. Getting your ideas out on paper quickly and then going back to edit will save you tons of time writing papers, and you can get through a lot of reading assignments by speed reading and pulling out the main ideas. Both skills will literally save you hours.

Finding what kind of work environment makes you the most productive is also important. Explore the different places on campus where you can do your work and find ways to make yourself more efficient, whether that means working with food, music, or company. Pandora (a personalized Internet radio service) was my savior on those long days and nights in the library. Sometimes I needed to add a little feeling of fun and putting Pandora on in the background helped me be more content with sitting still. Test out different methods and see how much you get done in each scenario. Efficiency is the key.

Whatever you choose to do, remember that going to college is an amazing opportunity that many people do not have available to them. You have to make the time worth it and honor those who don't have the privilege by taking it seriously and doing your best.

PROFESSORS 101

No matter how seriously you take college, you will inevitably encounter some difficult classes and professors.

The number one thing I can't stand in a classroom is when an instructor asks for a specific answer when there are so many different ways to look at the subject matter, and the "right" answer is really up for interpretation. Sometimes a professor will have a specific word or answer in mind, but that kind of thinking makes me feel completely trapped in a space in which I spend more time trying to figure out how to think the same as everyone else than I spend actually learning. I kind of shut down at that point.

That's a pet peeve of mine, but you may also have bigger problems. A truly dreadful professor, to me, is someone who doesn't teach me anything, who wastes my time, or who creates an environment of disrespect. Of course, I have felt all of those in one classroom or another, but never all at once. I dealt with each one accordingly. One class moved at an insultingly slow pace and although I knew how busy I was, I dropped out of it and added a more challenging class because good grades were less important to me than being challenged. In required classes that I felt were a waste of time, I multitasked and did other things to maintain my sanity like drawing, brainstorming for my next art piece, or reading.

Good grades were less important to me than being challenged.

Even though there's a lot that can go wrong with class, there's also a lot that can go right. Many professors are more than happy to speak with students about the struggles they are having, and help out. College is unique because it surrounds you with other students who are in the same position that you are in, and with professors who are available to you and willing to teach you what they know. Take advantage of those infrastructures and look within them for the answers. But also remember that college is about thinking outside of the obvious options that are available, and making your own experience what you want it to be.

COLLEGE LIFE

WORK

Look for university jobs. There are a lot of fun ways to pick up some extra cash on campus. Many schools have psychology departments in need of volunteers for studies. It's an interesting, potentially fun way to earn some extra money. Also, for any artist, being a monitor in the photo lab, the woodshop, or metal shop is a dream job: you get paid for studio time!

MEETING NEW PEOPLE

It was interesting to see and encounter all the different types of people in a college environment, from the stereotypical male jocks, ditsy girls, and nerds, to everyone in between and on the outskirts. But all of us were the same in a lot of ways, too, because we were all fighting for a place in a competitive world. Whether it was to prove something to ourselves or our families, or we were fighting some other battle, we were all working for something, and carving out a place of our own. Observing this taught me a lot about the common human experience of playing the game and trying to make it out alive. All over the world, that's what people are doing: trying to stay happy, stay afloat, forget, remember, and live in peace. It's no different in college.

ROOMMATES

I had two roommates during my freshman year. The first one transferred out after the first semester, which shows that she was unhappy. I did what I could to help her, but I spent more time in other parts of campus than in my room for my own sanity. It was difficult for me to adjust to a whole new life when someone I was around all of the time was depressed.

My second roommate was a good friend whom I met during the first semester. Surprisingly, living with a friend was almost more difficult! I was happier in my dorm room with her, but I got a lot less done and that added stress. We were also comfortable being in each other's space, and that lack of boundaries changed the level of privacy we had. But, living in such close quarters, you have to sacrifice something. In the end, although my second roommate and I had more difficulty working out boundaries than my first roommate and I did, sacrificing privacy for laughter was worth it for me.

MAKING FRIENDS AND FORGING RELATIONSHIPS

Don't live on your phone. Be as present as possible. Allow yourself to feel uncomfortable. Talk to as many people in your classes and in your dorm as you can. Do the things that you love and branch out by trying things that spark your interest; that's how you'll be able to make lasting friends and create the life you want in school.

> I thought that I was strong coming out of high school, but my high school experience didn't prepare me for what was to come.

I loved going for night hikes. Going out for dinner is always a good time. Get off campus and check out a concert, a poetry slam, or a movie. Whatever you do, get a group of people together and just have fun. Following your own passions and interests will lead you to friendships and make you feel more oriented than anything else.

The friendships that you form will be hugely important. You need friends to help you make it through college, and be glad that you did. It's a huge period of change in your life. I thought that I was strong coming out of high school, but my high school experience didn't prepare me for what was to come. Change *will* happen: within yourself, within your interpersonal relationships, in your mind, and in your passions. You will even experience physical change: your body will change, whether you gain or lose weight, or your posture shifts from the new weight on your shoulders. But if you have solid friends and good relationships, they will help you through all those difficult transitions.

TAKING CARE OF YOURSELF

Don't disregard your de-stressors. Know what makes you feel good, whether it's playing music, being active, or writing, and be sure to save a little time in your schedule for that.

Sleep is often sacrificed, and that is a huge issue. You will have sleepless nights, undoubtedly, but try to sleep when you can because it'll help with your memory, focus, social life, and maintaining your weight.

Most importantly, I have to stress how important it is that you be careful and protect yourself, both physically and emotionally. Everyone wants to be able to let go and trust. But keep in mind that if you make a mistake, you will have to deal with the struggles that follow, and they will weigh on you and on your progress.

I learned that lesson the hard way. I allowed a poisonous person into my life who infected some friendships that I will now never revive. The situation exhausted people I loved who didn't need to be exposed to that harm in their lives. Please, be careful and protect yourself.

THE ART OF EATING

Keep in mind what you probably already know: we need water more than anything to survive. Not to mention, if you're dehydrated, you'll eat more. Do an occasional grocery run, and keep snacks in your room and in your bag when going to class, which will keep you full longer. Don't let yourself get ravenous or when you hit the dorms, you'll binge, slopping pudding on top of omelets, without knowing why.

You can eat healthily in the dorms, but if you can't bear to gulp down some of the dorm veggies that you need, when you go out to eat be sure to make a conscious effort to order foods with the nutrients you're lacking.

Don't let yourself get ravenous or when you hit the dorms, you'll binge, slopping pudding on top of omelets, without knowing why.

As a side note, keep in mind that you can always go back for more food in the cafeteria. No one likes waiting on a line twice, but the amount of food we waste in dorms in horrendous and disgusting.

NO REGRETS

I once dropped out of an art class when I was at my ultimate low. I was in the middle of quitting something I loved—my sport, running—and I was deeply involved in an abusive relationship. I was on the brink of dropping out of college and my whole family was up in arms, frantic, on the other side of the country. That kind of deep depression sucks all feeling from your body, and your mind blocks out any kind of thought other than sensory data. It's impossible to be creative.

At that point, my grades were already plummeting, and the art professor for that class was known to be one of the toughest. But, honestly, I think that if I had stayed in that class, I would have had to push myself with art in a way that I haven't yet. Sometimes I wish I would have stuck it out.

I also wish I had studied abroad. I didn't ever waver from my sport when I was running, but looking back now I see that I was jailing myself in a way. My body was spent, and I was constantly fighting injury and that held me back from a lot of things, including studying abroad.

I'm out of school and broke now. I know that people don't necessarily stay in one location because they don't know where to go or don't know how to dream. It may be that they are stuck, financially. I'm afraid that's going to be my fate, that I'm not going to get to see as much as I want to because I can't afford it. The financial support that you can get to help you study abroad is really unique, and I wish I had taken advantage of that.

A lot of things didn't turn out the way I wanted or expected them to in college. There were a lot of big changes and developments for me. It wasn't easy in any way whatsoever, but I wouldn't change a thing about it. The things that aren't perfect about college are exactly what make the experience valuable.

DISCOVERING YOUR PASSIONS

College is the time to seek out what you are interested in. If a whole range of things interests you, that's ok. If nothing interests you, you have to try and figure out why. I was a mix of both: I wanted to learn everything, but there wasn't one thing pulling me more than any other, so it all felt somewhat neutral to me.

I've come to terms with that feeling of neutrality since graduating, because I have learned that I will work hard no matter what I do. So I have to make sure that I put that energy into something that is worthwhile and means something for *me*, because I won't get that self-satisfaction from anyone but myself.

I tried to keep that in mind when I chose my major, too. I decided to be one of "those people" who doesn't care about where the money is. It's not really glamorous either way, whether you're making money or not, but it's a decision you'll face at some point. And you'll have to deal with the consequences one way or another, either while you are in school or after you graduate, like I am now. But I don't regret doing what I love: making art.

AFTER YOU GRADUATE

There are some things that you can expect to leave college with: an understanding of time and its worth; how to prioritize; some feelings of incompetency; and a taste of academic competition. And there are things that you shouldn't expect to come out of college with: a job; a pat on the back; or connections that will lead you directly where you are meant to go. But what I think you absolutely *need* by the time you graduate is to be confident enough in your own body to make decisions as they come. And to realize that you don't know it all, but you do have the thirst to learn. Through everything, your mind and your heart will be your allies, and you will be able to keep moving onward.

EXPECTATIONS

Expect to leave college with:

- An understanding of the value of time
- How to prioritize
- Some feelings of incompetency
- A taste of academic competition

Don't expect to leave college with:

- A job
- A pat on the back
- A clear-cut path that will lead you directly where you are meant to go

If you told me while I was in college that after I graduated I would walk across Colorado, that I would move to San Francisco, I would just wonder, *why*? Now that I have graduated, things are not at all what I expected, but I'm still myself, I'm still going on adventures, and I just have to remember that there is no one, clear-cut pathway to where you want your life to go. I still don't know exactly where I'm headed, but what I do know is that this life is changing me in ways that wouldn't happen in school.

Graduating without knowing what you want is something every college student hopes *won't* happen to them. We think we should know exactly what we want to do, and many people around us constantly affirm that idea. You can't figure it all out on cue, and you will drive yourself crazy trying to. Create a more flexible vision of who you want to become, accept the things that you cannot control, and roll with it. ★

For more from Aislinn go to
www.nowyoutellmebooks.com/college.

LUCAS PAEZ

"It's your time. Your money. Your mind."

A biomedical engineering major at Rensselaer Poly-technic Institute, Lucas is no stranger to hitting the books, but also understands that the real value of a college education isn't measured by your GPA, but by the quality of your experience. Lucas has taken this approach in his own education, and has made his experience memorable by joining the Philippine American League and taking up a minor in psychology. Incidentally, he also survived a class taught by a "human-eating succubus."

COLLEGE LEARNING

CHOOSING A SCHOOL, CHOOSING A MAJOR

Rensselaer Polytechnic Institute was a good fit for me. To this day, I feel that going here is one of the best decisions I've ever made. It's far enough away from home, but close enough that I can choose to visit on any given weekend. It has a good reputation as an engineering school. It has my major, biomedical engineering, and has a large variety of courses available within the major, which is important to me.

I decided on biomedical engineering because the thought of being a med student was too daunting for me. Jokes aside, I was decent at math and sciences during high school, so I wanted to go into something that involved those skills and was something that I actually enjoyed doing. Basically, I picked out what I enjoyed and was interested in from high school, and looked into majors that correlated with those interests. And here I am.

Researching majors helps a lot. Look into what exactly you'll be studying, what courses you'll be taking, and what you can expect to do as an occupation later. Talking to professors is one of the best ways to collect more knowledge about potential majors. There is no better resource than someone who is already in the field or has already gotten their degree within your major, and they are usually willing to help you out. Who knows, they may even teach you a trick or two they've learned over the years, or secrets that only an experienced individual would know.

SECRETS TO ACADEMIC SUCCESS

Go to class. This may seem like a petty point to make, but it really cannot be emphasized enough. Unless it is absolutely necessary that you be absent, you should be going to each and every one of your classes. Sure, you may be able to borrow someone's notes, but you don't want to fall into a habit of missing class, especially when difficult work arrives. Once you miss a class due to sleeping in or whatnot, it becomes increasingly easier to miss subsequent classes, and that is a slippery slope you do not want to go down. You're not at college for a four-year-long vacation, and you didn't spend hundreds on textbooks just to skip class. Learn something.

Use the library as often as you can. For studying. *And that's it.* No looking at random pictures on the Internet, no casual instant messaging, just you and your course work. If you keep the library as a sacred place where you will always study and *only* study, you'll get into the good habit of using it when you need to really focus and crack down on something. Your room may seem like an adequate studying space because it's comfortable, but that's exactly the reason why it *shouldn't* be used for study. In addition to the obvious surrounding noise, you do more than just study when you're in your room, so you can be distracted much quicker. If you have a study haven like the library, your productivity will increase, especially when something absolutely needs to get done.

Office hours. Use them. *Even when you don't need to go.* Office hours more often than not end up being free, private tutoring sessions, and your professors will be more willing to help you with course work when you visit them on a constant basis. And don't be too proud or embarrassed to go get help if you're struggling. It's much better to be humbled and get an A than be cocky and pick up a C. Professors and teaching assistants are there for a reason: they know the subject better than you do, and they only want to see you do well. Professors will remember that you're making a genuine effort to learn, and will reward you for that effort. Plus, going

> **Office hours more often than not end up being free, private tutoring sessions.**

to office hours may be one of the smartest things to do in college, not only because getting to know and being friendly with your professors or teaching assistants can give you an academic advantage, but it can also open professional doors to research and other opportunities for work.

Stay organized. This is a personal preference, but I would also suggest using a single notebook for all of your classes, and different colored pens for each subject. It keeps your bag light and lets you have everything in one spot, instantly available, at any time.

Sit in the front. It's a small move that can have a big impact. You'll pay much more attention to the teacher, especially in big classes, where the otherwise distracting crowd of people behind you will seem to disappear.

PROFESSORS 101

I've always believed that a big part of your grades in college depends on your teacher. If your professor or teaching assistant is kind and helpful, you'll likely do well. On the flip side, if you really like the material you're learning but hate your professor with the fire of a thousand suns, you may struggle. It's fair to say that it's inevitable that you'll have at least one professor that you'll absolutely despise.

I once had a biology professor who was a complete human-eating succubus. Even though bio was one of my favorite subjects, the course was a nightmare because of the professor. She would make fun of us during class, laugh audibly whenever someone asked a question she thought was stupid, and was generally unwilling to help her students. In addition, the teaching assistants for the class were her minions, mimicking her every move and almost as unhelpful as she was. In cases like that, the best option is to team up with classmates and friends to get through the class together, which is what I did. We scheduled weekly study sessions and homework reviews, and crammed for exams together. Using all of your resources will not only help you through class work, but will help keep you sane, too. You can't do this alone.

COLLEGE IS NOT AN EXTENSION OF HIGH SCHOOL

You know that awful feeling when you get a poor grade on a test? That's your body telling you that you need to study harder next time. Use that as motivation to become more effort oriented than you ever were in high school. How? Focus on actually learning the material, rather than just getting a good grade. It's much better to know the information in the field you're pursuing and get a B than to not absorb anything and get an A.

Even if you study hard, you *will* fail a few exams in college. It doesn't matter how good your grades were in high school, it will happen. This is mostly because some professors want to challenge you, and weed out the students that aren't willing to take college work seriously. You *will* have to study much more than you did in high school, so get used to it and accept it.

Your college years will be some of the best years of your life, but they'll also be the most challenging ones. That goes not only for school-work, but for figuring out who you are and how you are growing as a person. No matter what college you go to, and what circumstances you are in, you will grow during these years.

> **No matter what college you go to, and what circumstances you are in, you will grow during these years.**

COLLEGE LIFE

STRIKING THE BALANCE

There's a popular saying that tells college students they can pick only two out of these three choices: good grades, a social life, and adequate sleep. I've found this generalization to be somewhat true, and if you add dating or romance in there, you're only allowed to pick one other. If you have the energy and time for casual dating, by all means, go for it! You'll meet some absolutely wonderful people. Just be prepared to lose time out of your normal schedule or routine if you do.

I have to state, though, that sleep is *so* important. Getting your normal quota of sleep, whether it is six hours or nine hours, is crucial once work starts piling on. You'll be more focused during the day, you won't have to depend on caffeine to keep you going, and ultimately you'll be more productive.

Whatever you decide to do with your time, please, please, please don't complain and moan when you don't have enough time for everything. You make your schedule and you have to deal with it. It shouldn't be anyone's problem but yours.

LET PEOPLE IN

Bring a doorstop! During your freshman year, people will be coming in and out of your room often. Floormates and others will generally be willing to stop and introduce themselves if they see that you are willing to let others into your room. And trust me on this: your floor during freshman year almost becomes family. You're in this together, and you will find it very difficult to get by alone. Leave your door open whenever possible. Well, except when you're sleeping.

PARTYING

Be prepared to have the most freedom you've ever had, and be prepared to feel overwhelmed at times by that newfound freedom. Almost everyone parties, especially during freshman year when college life is new to everyone, but some students are prone to abusing their freedom. Use this time to meet new people, have some fun, and step out of your comfort zone when you can, but realize that you are now developing fully as an individual and you must not only treat others with complete kindness, but treat yourself and your body with consideration and respect, as well.

Really, too many times I've seen freshmen come into college with no idea how to handle themselves in regard to alcohol, and they end up puking all over the floor or even being taken to the hospital. Drinking too much can happen at times, but you need to make sure that it doesn't happen *every* time you drink. If you're vomiting most times you drink, guess what: you're doing something terribly wrong. I know it may seem like consuming alcohol in moderation is an obvious precaution, but you really need to be conscious of it at all times. If you learn how to drink and handle alcohol appropriately, you'll have more fun.

A famous quote from James Thurber sums it up well: "One martini is all right. Two are too many, and three are not enough." Know your limits, and don't forget that you're responsible for all of your actions.

BE KIND

At college, you'll meet people from all around the world. Learn from them, and they'll learn from you. Treat everyone with ultimate kindness. Make eye contact and smile genuinely at people when you see them. As a general rule, be extra nice to the secretary, janitor, cashiers, and other workers. Know them by name and engage in conversation with them when you can. Everyone's story is different, and if you take the time to genuinely listen to those stories, and to notice the people who usually go unnoticed, your life will be the better for it. Plus, many times, they hold the real power within an office or department and can help you out when you dearly need it.

Be extra nice to the secretary, janitor, cashiers, and other workers. If you take the time to notice the people who usually go unnoticed, your life will be the better for it.

Another thing I've learned is that it's okay to suck up to people sometimes; it's okay to try extra hard to show someone that you respect them. Your superiors are called that for a reason: they usually have the things that you need or want. Sometimes you have to try a little harder in order to get those things.

MANAGING TECHNOLOGY SO IT DOESN'T MANAGE YOU

In this age, it is easy to fall into the technology trap in which our lives revolve around and are defined by our computers: our contacts, e-mails, bank accounts, music, and class work can often all be found on our computers. My biggest mistake during my college career was having my computer open almost whenever I had spare time. It was nearly a default setting for me; if I had nothing else to do, I would have the Internet open and do . . . absolutely nothing. Looking back, I regret that I let myself fall into that technology trap, and I wish I had made more of an effort to go outside, try new things, or do things as simple as talking to someone new I hadn't met yet or riding a bicycle.

The same goes for academics. If possible, avoid bringing your laptop to class. Obviously, if it's a computer-aided class, you have no choice, but if you do have the choice, it's best not to have the distraction of a computer at your fingertips. Take notes using a notebook and a pen instead. If you have a computer screen in front of you during class, it basically acts as a wall between you and the professor, and that makes it nearly impossible to pay attention and absorb information.

I go to a tech school, so naturally I've seen quite a few people fall victim to one of the biggest technology traps of all time: video games. Don't get me wrong, video games are loads of fun and are a great relaxation tool. However, serious gamers may sometimes develop an addiction to a game, causing them to waste a lot of time in college when they could be doing other things.

The experiences that you'll have in real life will trump any shallow experiences that you'll have playing a video game. Try new things; you'll regret it later on if you don't. You only go to college once.

AND MOST IMPORTANTLY . . .

- These are your four years. No one else's. It's your time. Your money. Your mind. So strive not to let yourself be bothered by what other people think about you. When you start doing that, you are no longer yourself, but the creation of others.

- Don't hide who you really are. Your true personality will eventually come to the surface anyway. Remember who you are, why you chose to be here, and just be yourself.

- You are young and can do practically anything you want. So you need to have an open mind coming into college; take risks you normally wouldn't take.

- Don't force yourself into doing something you don't want to do. If you don't want to go out and party one night, don't do it. If you don't want to join a fraternity, don't get pressured into doing it. Always do what *you* want to do.

- Call your parents when you can. You've lived your whole life knowing they were always there. One day they won't be.

- Don't stress about anything that happens in college. Worrying about trivial stuff only intensifies stress. College is so small when you look at the big picture: it's just another four years of your life. At the same time, four years is a long time to be unhappy and stressing out. So just be happy, laugh, make memories, and smile. ★

For more from Lucas go to
www.nowyoutellmebooks.com/college.

NICOLE BARRON

"Find the time to laugh and have a little fun!"

Ballroom-dancing, American Sign Language–practicing Nicole attends New York University, her "dream school." NYU was everything she hoped it would be, although the process of declaring a major was not at all like she had expected. Now a journalism major, Nicole has come up with some creative ways to get a hold of expensive textbooks, and creative ways to make her college experience count.

COLLEGE LEARNING

THE COST OF COLLEGE LIVING

Fact: college kids love free stuff. We're all on a tight budget, so it's great when you can find freebies or great discounts. The first place you should look for free stuff is on your own campus. Colleges are full of free food and giveaways, especially at the beginning of the year when clubs give out free food in order to attract potential members. Even if you're not really interested in joining a club, grab a bite of whatever they're handing out anyway. While you're eating, you might find out that you're interested in what the club has to offer after all!

Another way to find free stuff is to embrace the idea of "freeganism." Dorms are great places to grab the stuff that other students don't want and are just going to throw out, especially at the end of the school year when everyone is cleaning out their rooms. I've gotten a full-length mirror, a dish-drying rack, and some nonperishable foods. I'm not saying you have to go dumpster diving, just keep an eye out for those freebies.

You definitely don't have to spend like crazy to live well at college.

Besides looking for free stuff, you can also look for great discounts. Lately, discount websites like LivingSocial have been gaining more and more popularity, and these are great resources. You can find offers and discounts for haircuts, trips, restaurants, and tons more. It's also a good idea to check out stores on or near your campus, because some of them may give discounts to college students. You definitely don't have to spend like crazy to live well at college.

TEN TEXTBOOKS FOR ONE CLASS? THIS BOOK COSTS *HOW* MUCH?

Buying my own textbooks was definitely a huge change for me. I went to a public high school, and while the textbooks weren't in the best condition, I didn't pay for them, so I couldn't complain. So seeing the book lists when I got to college was definitely a shock.

There's nothing like looking at a syllabus and seeing that the professor has listed ten books for the class. It's also not fun to see that the price tag on the science textbook you need says "two hundred dollars." And on top of that, you'll have to buy books for at least two or three other classes.

I spent hundreds of dollars on books for three semesters until I said "enough is enough" and got creative. My trick was going where the books are always free: the library. College libraries are huge and almost always have the books that you'll need for your classes in their collection. Borrowing a book for free and then returning it? That sounded like my kind of deal. The only downside to this system, however, is that most college libraries will pull class books into the reserve section of the library at the request of the professor. This prevents students from hogging all the library books for a class and not allowing others to use them. Once books are on reserve, there will probably be a time limit: at my school, you can only check out a reserve book for two hours at a time.

It may seem like you won't be able to get any work done in just two hours, but I've found that it's the exact opposite. Because I'm on a tight deadline, I know that I have to get work done during those two hours or else I'll have just wasted that two-hour rental period. Plus, two hours of hard work with one book is definitely enough for me. After two hours it's nice to move on to another subject or take a break entirely.

If the library doesn't have a book you need, then you'll have to buy it. But no one says that you have to spend full price. Look around for used books. Does it really matter if there's some writing on the pages if you just saved fifty bucks? Also, look for websites that rent out textbooks, like chegg.com. One of the worst things at the end of a semester is trying to figure out what you're going to do with a bunch of textbooks you'll never need again. That's why renting is so great: you just send the books back when you're finished with the class, and it usually costs much less than buying them.

TO DO WORK OR NOT TO DO WORK?

This is a question that I ask myself every day. A great thing about college is that you don't have a parent or teacher standing over you and bugging you about whether or not you've finished your homework. In fact, there really isn't anyone telling you to do your homework. While some professors will mention that you have homework due, others really don't care if you do your homework at all. So basically it's all up to you. It's up to you to make the time to sit down and work, to go to the library, and to remember to turn in your assignments.

In one sense, the college work load is less than what you got in high school, but in another sense it's way more. There's less homework in the sense that you won't have an assignment due every day for every class: you might only have one assignment due per week for each class. But that one assignment isn't just some dinky worksheet; it could be a seven-page essay that might take you hours to write. You really need to plan when you're going to make time to do that work.

THE PITFALLS OF PROCRASTINATION: FACEBOOK AND NAPS AND YOUTUBE! OH MY!

Once you plan out a time when you're going to do your homework, you have to avoid the many pitfalls of procrastination. Procrastination is definitely something that I struggle with all the time when it comes to homework and studying.

One of my biggest enemies when I'm trying to do work is the lure of the nap. I love naps; I don't think you'll find a college student who doesn't. Sleep is hard to come by in college and you have to take advantage of it when you can. So I'll often tell myself that taking an hour-long nap won't be *that* bad and I'll still have hours and hours to study . . . and then my one-hour nap turns into a three-hour nap. The key to napping is that you have to really limit your nap time. Make sure you set an alarm and make sure your hand doesn't find the snooze button when it goes off.

On the other hand, it's important to be able to recognize when your body *needs* to take a nap break. Sometimes when I'm studying I find that my eyelids are starting to close and that the words are beginning to blur even though I've been "reading" for the last five minutes. If you know that you're too tired to be productive anyway, take a twenty-minute nap. After a quick power nap you'll be energized and ready to get your work done rather than wasting an hour staring at a piece of paper.

Another enemy is the Internet. When I'm avoiding homework, I find myself playing some game, browsing Facebook

I'll often tell myself that taking an hour-long nap won't be that bad and I'll still have hours and hours to study . . . and then my one-hour nap turns into a three-hour nap.

or YouTube, or going on a website that I haven't been on in years. It's up to you to just say no when you really have to get work done, but if you can't say no, which I usually can't, try this app called SelfControl. SelfControl allows you to block websites that you know will draw you away from homework, and you can block them for one to twenty-four hours. If you can't say no, let your computer say no for you!

COLLEGE LIFE

MAKING SCHOOL LIFE FIT *YOUR* LIFE

One of the biggest differences between high school and college is the type of classes that are offered in college. There is so much more variety in college. Instead of a general global history class, you'll find classes dedicated to the histories of Russia, the Gulf War, Mesopotamia, the Incan civilization, and the Silk Road, just to name a few. The variety is nice, but it also adds stress when you are picking classes, because there are so many choices!

The vast increase in the number of available classes allows you to take classes that really interest you. Unlike in high school, you won't have this preplanned schedule that tells you what classes to take and when. But it goes both ways. Because you can choose what interests you, you might find out that a class that sounded really interesting at first is actually something that you don't want to take at all. That happens and that's okay. That happened to me my first semester, and I dropped the class right away and registered for something else. The great thing about college is that you can switch your schedule if it's not really what you want. You should be happy with the classes that you are taking.

You should also take classes that interest you in order to fulfill requirements. That's how I ended up taking American Sign Language. I needed to fulfill a foreign language requirement but had always had a hard time memorizing vocabulary words, even English ones! So my academic adviser suggested that I might do better in ASL since I'd be remembering hand motions instead of spoken words. It proved to be true and I'm still having a lot of fun in ASL fulfilling my language requirement. So much fun, actually, that I made it my minor!

NICOLE'S DORM ESSENTIALS

- Bed risers
- Can opener
- Extra-long twin bed sheets
- Microwave
- Microwave-safe cups and dishes
- Mini-fridge
- Mirror
- Pictures of family and friends
- Shower caddy
- Silverware
- Stain remover
- Storage containers
- Water bottle

For a more comprehensive list, visit nowyoutellmebooks.com/college.

DON'T CHOOSE YOUR MAJOR LIKE I DID

When I look back at how and when I declared my journalism major, I think I should have waited. During orientation I had a break in my schedule, so I went to the Journalism Department to ask some questions about a class and I came out having declared my major. That's right, I declared my major before I even started college. Even though I felt very confident in pursuing journalism, I still don't really know why I declared so early. Luckily, it worked out for me in the end, because I still love my major two years later.

My decision could have gone horribly wrong, though, if it turned out that I hated journalism, so I would definitely recommend taking at least one class, if not many more, in your major before you make a decision. Even if you feel as confident as I did, you just never know.

GYM? WHAT GYM?

It's important to keep your mind *and* your body healthy in college. But you don't have to go to the gym every day to stay healthy. Sure, the gym is a great place to get exercise, and for many people it might be the best option. But for people like me, there are other great forms of exercise that you can explore.

I've been a member of the Ballroom and Latin Dance Team at NYU since the fall of my freshman year. Dancing is a fun way to get that exercise into your schedule, and it doesn't even feel like you're exercising at all! You're just having fun and learning something new.

Another great way to get exercise is by biking. I bike everywhere. When you have a bike, you don't have to wait for public or school transportation, you don't have to walk, and you don't get stuck in traffic. I ride through the city and come across traffic all the time, but I never get held up. I just zoom through all the cars and trucks knowing that I'll get to my destination before they do. My legs have gotten so strong from riding my bike, and I'm now in better shape than I was in high school!

FINDING FRIENDS

You will *constantly* be meeting new people at college. Sure, you'll meet the largest number of new people at the beginning of your freshman year, but there will always be more people that you haven't met.

Finding friends out of all the people you'll meet is a big concern for a lot of students, but especially freshmen. As a freshman, you're coming to a school where you don't know anyone and are anxious to find friends. But you might find that the people who thought you'd be friends with won't really turn out to be your friends in the end. I thought I'd be friends with a group of students I met at orientation. We would hang out, stay up all night, and go to eat together. Between orientation and the beginning of the school year, we wrote on each other's Facebook walls, talked about classes and dorms, and planned on meeting up when school started. But I never saw any of them, and I know that a lot of my friends now had the same thing happen to them as freshmen.

Don't stress out too much about finding friends, because you will find them. You'll find the people that you'll be able to study with, go to parties with, take pictures with, and with whom you can make great and lasting memories. It happens naturally if you just be yourself!

ROOMMATES

An important thing to remember is that you don't have to be best friends with your roommate. A lot of people come to college thinking they're going to hang out with their roommate and that they're always going to go out and do things together. I thought that, too. Sometimes that does happen and that's great, but you have to realize that not everyone will mesh and you don't *have* to be best friends. If you can live together and be civil, then that's a successful match.

If you and your roommate can just live together and be civil, then that's a successful match.

Even if you live with a friend with whom you get along with really well, there will be some adjustment. And you'll both have to compromise, too. It's not just your room; it's a room for two or three or more people. Compromise is a part of living with a roommate and it's part of life.

YOU AND YOUR COLLEGE YEARS

The years you spend in college will be unlike any other years in your life, because there are so many things that you can get out of college that will affect your future. You may get a degree in something that you love or something that you hate. You may find lifelong friends or friends that you'll slowly lose touch with over the years. You may find the love of your life or someone that you realize you don't want to be with. There are so many things that you can get out of college, and those things will be different for everyone.

But to get the most out of college, you have to be yourself, know yourself, and work hard. Know your interests and know that it's okay to change your plans. Avoid the people that don't look out for you and your well-being. Study hard but also take breaks. Keep an open mind, learn from your mistakes, and most importantly, find time to laugh and have a little fun! ★

For more from Nicole go to
www.nowyoutellmebooks.com/college.

BONUS MATERIAL

JANE ADAMS

"Make it pay!"

J ane first began her undergraduate education at
Missouri State University in 1988. She enjoyed her
course work, but life soon intervened, and, as a single
mother of a young son, Jane chose to put school on the back
burner. Now, as a forty-four-year-old, full-time student, she's
back and better than ever.

HOW IT ALL BEGAN

Missouri State University is located in Springfield, Missouri, where I live; I'm a local. It was my hometown school when I was twenty-one, and it still is at forty-four. It's a big university, with about seventeen thousand students on the Springfield campus. Still, choosing Missouri State is not a compromise for me; I didn't "settle" for it. I truly enjoy attending MSU. I find that it offers a good education at a reasonable cost.

Prior to returning to school, I had a good job as a bookkeeper and was making good money. I was earning the best living that a woman without a college degree can get in Springfield, Missouri. But I had reached my maximum earning potential at that job; there was no expectation of upward advancement, nowhere to go. I had a choice: either be satisfied with the earning limitations or go back and get my degree. And if I chose the latter, it had to be "now or never!"

My husband and I made a deliberate choice when I opted for the degree. To make it work, we minimized our bills and watched our finances carefully, because as a full-time student, I'm no longer bringing in an income. But college is my priority: that's the key to success.

COLLEGE LEARNING

CHOOSING A MAJOR

I'm a practical person. I have returned to school with one goal in mind: to obtain a degree that will enable me to get an excellent job.

When I was at Missouri State in my early twenties, I chose an English major; however, when I returned to school, I decided to select a major that would provide a solid foundation for the career I wanted to pursue.

When I came back to MSU, I studied accounting and economics but settled on an economics major for two reasons. First, I have a natural understanding of the subject matter; it makes sense to me. Second, the economics degree will qualify me for the particular job that I would love to have, either in banking or for an agency that regulates financial institutions. I want to apply what I'm learning. I want a career that not only pays well, but that also provides me with a challenge, that makes me think every day.

> **I want to apply what I'm learning. I want a career that not only pays well, but that also provides me with a challenge, that makes me think every day.**

JOB COMPETITION

I'm not worried about the job market. Granted, there will be a lot of young people on the market, but most employers will hire me over them. I already have experience in the workplace; I'm older, and also more mature, stable, and dependable. This gives me a leg up over young kids who are fresh out of school.

THE TUITION TAB

A person who is considering returning to college as an older, "nontraditional" student might be intimidated by the prospect of a big tuition expense, but that may not be a problem. In my case, I'm not paying out-of-pocket for my education. I am the recipient of two grants and a scholarship, so I'm not actually paying anything to go back to school—not one dime.

Before I decided to return to school, I researched where I could go to get grants and scholarships to pay for tuition. Otherwise, my husband and I couldn't afford it, particularly since I'd be leaving my job to go to school full-time.

There are lots of scholarships and grants available, if people explore the possibilities. The Pell Grant I'm receiving is part of a program that Missouri State offers for returning students. To apply for the Pell Grant, you fill out a form online. The WIA grant was part of the stimulus package, and I applied for that through the Missouri Career Center. They interviewed me, I showed them a course projection plan, and I was approved.

Missouri State has so many scholarships that it recently revamped its scholarship page on its website because kids were missing out on scholarship and grant opportunities. There are 759 different scholarships available. Now, at MSU, you go online, fill out one application, and the university will process it; it automatically forwards your application to every scholarship that you qualify for.

The fact that I'm here on scholarship and grants has contributed to my academic performance. Part of the reason I have a 4.0 is that I have to answer to people; if I wasn't making a 4.0, they might reconsider! I want to show them that I'm not wasting their money.

SECRETS TO ACADEMIC SUCCESS

Scheduling class work and keeping on top of studies and assignments is easier for me than it is for the average college student. As a mature adult, I have spent many years working in a very responsible position, and I've become accustomed to working without direct supervision. This translates easily into keeping up with my class work without someone standing over me.

Go to class. One thing I would definitely recommend is that students attend class every day. You'll have a much easier time making your grades if you follow this one simple rule: go to class, no matter what. You have to make college your priority if you want to succeed. To do well, you have to show up.

Sit in the front. When you are choosing the seat that you'll occupy all semester long, don't follow the other folks as they head toward the back of the classroom; do the smart thing, the adult thing, and sit in the front of the class. Why? It's easier to hear, easier to see, and easier to get the instructor's attention when you need it.

Pay attention. I'm lucky: I have an excellent memory. But if you're not paying attention to what the professor is talking about, what difference would your memory make? Remember: you've paid good money to take this course. Pay attention to what the professor says so you can make the grade. Plus, you just might learn something.

Do the assignments before they're due. As soon as a task is assigned in class, I do it; it doesn't matter when it's due. I don't wait. If I have everything I need to perform the task, I go ahead and get it done. It's a comfort not having to worry about deadlines and late work; I like that.

Test dates should operate by the same standard: students should not wait until the last minute to study for an exam. I often see students delaying for so long that they're obliged to cram for the test, go without sleep, and try to absorb all the information at once. That's the road to disaster!

Create a good study environment. At home I have a study area where I keep everything I need to do my academics. I have a good desk space, and beside it there are shelves where I keep all my textbooks and notebooks. (I make a three-ring notebook for each class each semester, and everything from the course goes into the notebook: the syllabus, my class notes, any PowerPoint printouts, assignment sheets, supplemental readings, etc.) My computer and printer are set up there, too.

My workstation has everything I need to study, immediately at hand, which makes it easy to do my work. I don't waste time looking for a misplaced textbook, lost assignment sheets, or mislaid notes. I have it all in one organized spot.

Don't take on too much. One mistake I see students make is taking on too much. When students have a full class load, take a job, and throw a social life into the mix, they become overloaded and overwhelmed. That's a recipe for failure. When you are in college, whether you're a kid fresh out of high school or a middle-aged person like me, college must be your priority if you want to succeed.

Don't put your social life ahead of your academic goals. I see so many younger students blow off their studies in favor of socializing and romance. It's not that I don't get it; when I was nineteen, I was more interested in what I was doing on Saturday night than I was in what was happening in class, too. But now that I'm forty-four, I know what I'm doing on Saturday night: my homework.

> Clearly, it's my age that makes the difference. My clock is ticking louder; I don't have time to waste.

Clearly, it's my age that makes the difference. The young students are not as invested, in part, because they have all the time in the world: their whole lives are still ahead of them. Whereas I'm middle-aged, my clock is ticking louder; I don't have time to waste.

COLLEGE LIFE

HOW A RETURNING STUDENT DEALS WITH . . .

Roommates. As a mature student and a local resident, I avoided some of the adjustments and challenges that younger students face. I didn't have to adapt to dorm life or a new roommate; as a married woman, my husband makes a fine roommate, and I am already accustomed to his habits.

Food. Since I'm not eating the cafeteria food, I can't offer any advice on that front; I skipped the "freshman fifteen" and went straight to middle-aged spread, more's the pity. Anyway, one of the comforts of middle age is the consumption of fried food. I'm enjoying it while I can, because I know that someday my doctor will take it away from me.

Friends. In college and in life, friends should be people with whom you have things in common, and, moreover, people who can make you laugh.

I've made lots of friends on campus—friends of all ages. I walk from class to class with returning students, I have a standing lunch date with a nineteen-year-old student, and I've developed relationships with other kids from my classes, just talking and laughing on campus.

I don't know of any campus groups that are geared to older students, but that's not anything I need. I already had relationships in place before I came back to school: my husband, my friends, and my family. I'm not looking for social relationships, but I've enjoyed the people I've met.

Bad professors. Some of your professors will be better than others. When they know their subject, and love it, and can communicate well, you're in for a great experience. But that doesn't always happen.

I had one professor who, although he was a very nice person, was a horrible teacher. When that happens, what do you do? Study harder! I just dealt with it, and I had to study the textbook more thoroughly to make up for the lack of meaningful lecture material.

Challenges. Some of the aspects of college that seem difficult to adjust to initially will end up teaching you skills that will be useful later in life. At college you'll learn how to deal with bureaucracy, meet deadlines, manage your time, and be self-sufficient.

Scheduling concerns. If your return to college is going to be a success, you have to make college your priority. The amount of time that you have to devote to college is considerable: the time spent in class; time for homework, studying for exams, research; hours in the library. It's really important to avoid getting overloaded, because if you get overloaded, you're going to flunk.

I see other students who are coming back to school; and in addition to their academics, they are trying to work, and raise young families, and

> **Before you make the decision to return to school, sit down with your family, and make sure that they support the decision and can see that your education has to be a priority.**

maintain their homes, and cook and clean and cut the grass—it can be too much. Before you make the decision to return, sit down with your family, and make sure that they support the decision and can see that your education has to be a priority. My husband is so supportive, and it makes a big difference.

Also, people need to know what they can let go. So what if you didn't get the grass cut? Cut it next week. School is more important than the grass.

WHAT TO EXPECT

Come on. You need to be self-sufficient. As an adult, you must be able to support yourself. The end goal for every college student should be to get a degree that will enable you to make money: money to support your kids and yourself; to pay for your health insurance, your home, your car, your retirement. Money may not make you happy, but it will surely make you more comfortable.

And as a college student, you have the opportunity to get a degree in the area that interests you, and you have the opportunity to choose a career path that resonates with you. You're going to be at that job almost every day for the rest of your life, so it makes sense to qualify yourself to do something that you love. If you can be self-sufficient, doing what you love to do, you are living the good life.

WILL MY EDUCATION PAY OFF?

One question that all returning students should ask themselves before they decide to go back to school is: will it pay off? Look at the degree you really want to pursue, and decide whether it will make fiscal sense to return to school.

Education is always a good thing; I believe in education for its own sake. But at a certain age, putting your life on hold to go back to school doesn't make economic sense. You won't recoup your investment. At a certain age you are better off staying at your current job.

My degree is going to pay enough to justify quitting my job to go back to school because, in my case, I'll still have twenty to twenty-five work years left to make money with this degree.

Also, before you decide to return, ask yourself: Do I like school? Am I any good at it? It's a lot of money to throw away if you don't enjoy the process. And if you don't like it well enough to make the grades, then the sacrifice is not worthwhile.

Be sure you have the ability and the determination, because going back to school requires both. Though I love the course work in college, I'm in my mid-forties, and had worked behind a desk for years. Now I'm schlepping around in the wind and rain and cold, walking a mile from class to class; this is not something I'm used to. My backpack weighs thirty pounds! Young people can take it in stride, but I feel like a turtle. I dread the snow!

REGRETS

Obviously, I'm a pragmatist. I am not given to indulging in regrets or wasting time worrying about what might have been. Nonetheless, I confess that I regret not finishing college when I was young. People who get their degree when they are young have an advantage: they have more career choices because of their education. For example, I would have loved the chance to go into law; but at this stage in my life, I don't have the time to devote to graduate school and learning the profession from the ground up. As you age, you have less time to pursue your educational options.

JANE'S SECRETS TO ACADEMIC SUCCESS

- Go to class.
- Sit in the front.
- Pay attention.
- Do the assignments before they're due.
- Create a good study environment.
- Don't get overwhelmed.
- Don't put your social life ahead of your academic goals.

For more study tips, visit nowyoutellmebooks.com/college.

Moreover, if I'd finished my schooling, I would have earned more money. A degree translates into earning potential; and the sooner you have it, the sooner you earn it. You have the chance to start building for retirement.

My college experience would have been much different if I had gone when I was younger. I would have been involved in more college organizations, both academic and social. I would have liked to have joined a sorority when I was young, to see what that experience was like. It seems, as I look back, that it would have been fun to enjoy the friendships and the social aspect that a sorority offers. But it's too late now, obviously.

Admittedly, I wouldn't have been as good a student as I am now in my forties. My potential for success was there when I was younger: I was just as smart then as I am now! I had the talent, but I didn't pursue it because I was just as distracted as everyone else. Now that I'm older, my responsibilities and obligations have come into sharper focus. It's true what they say: with age comes wisdom.

But that's ancient history. Don't let it be said that I cry over spilled milk! I do not regret anything in my life, and it has led me to the comfortable and satisfying spot that I currently occupy. I'm striving to exemplify the triumphant return of the middle-aged student.

AND MOST IMPORTANTLY . . .

You are enjoying an opportunity right now that is important and valuable. Take it seriously! Work hard, pay attention, and plan for the future. Set a goal for your college education, and make that education pay off in the long run. ★

For more from Jane go to
www.nowyoutellmebooks.com/college.

KALEEN LONG

"It's not where you go, but who you are, that matters."

When Kaleen was transplanted from her small, Midwestern hometown to New Haven, Connecticut, she was overwhelmed, having graduating from a high school class of only twenty-seven. Now that she has graduated with degrees in English and Italian, Kaleen knows that choosing to attend Yale University was the right decision.

HOW IT ALL BEGAN

As a girl growing up in the Midwest, I attended a K–12 laboratory school located on the campus of the local state university, and each class was limited to thirty students. I was essentially a small-town girl, and a graduate of a tiny high school, when I arrived on the Yale campus in New Haven, Connecticut.

COLLEGE LEARNING

CHOOSING A SCHOOL

My high school counselor advised me to apply not only to schools where I could be confident that I'd get a letter of acceptance, but also to a "reach" school as well: a school that is very selective, that everyone is trying to get into. I decided to apply to Yale. I knew I couldn't bank on it, but I wanted to try; you never know what might happen.

I don't know for sure what it was about my application that got me in. You never know exactly what they seek: unique people from different backgrounds, I guess. I wrote two essays as part of my application, and I talked about my experience in a smaller high school. I had lots of activities; going to a small high school offers the chance to be involved in many things.

It's really not where you go but who you are that matters. A good student will be successful whether they go to a famous Ivy League school, or a state university, or a small, private college.

When I got accepted, I couldn't pass up the opportunity to go.

I truly enjoyed being at Yale; I believe I was meant to be there. It's an experience I would not wish to change. Still, I don't take the position that the Ivy League is the only way to go or the only key to getting a great education. I try to tell people all the time that it's really not where you go but who you are that matters. A good student will be successful whether he or she goes to a famous Ivy League school, or a state university, or a small private college. If you have a genuine interest in learning, work hard, and are willing to put yourself out there to meet new people, you will have a great college experience.

CHOOSING A MAJOR

Originally, I was planning on pursuing a premed path and majoring in science. However, I realized my freshman year that, at that point in my education, I didn't really want to be in a lab all day, every day. I took a literature class my freshman year that was absolutely wonderful, so I decided to take more English classes. I loved the reading, preferred my English classes over all others, so for my major, I went with what I loved to do.

In my junior year my intermediate Italian professor encouraged me to continue my studies and complete the major, so I did, and earned a degree in Italian, too.

Now I'm applying to medical school, but I don't regret the study of literature and Italian. Back when I was considering which area to major in, I sought advice from doctors I know, and they told me, "Don't be afraid to branch out." Some said that even when you intend to go to medical school after graduation, you should study something else in undergrad because once you get to medical school, it's all science all the time.

GREAT PROFESSORS, GREAT CLASSES

The class that made the biggest impression on me was Victorian Fiction and British Art. In addition to assigning great classics to read, the course wove art appreciation into the experience in a fabulous way.

Yale has the Yale Center for British Art, which holds great works of art by British masters. Each week we would discuss a novel we had read and then follow up that discussion by meeting at the art center to discuss a painting and see how it might relate to the reading we'd done. What an opportunity: to experience literature and the visual arts together. I saw William Blake's etchings!

SECRETS TO ACADEMIC SUCCESS

Keep up with your academics by doing your work every day; that way you won't have to cram. I'm not a Red Bull, caffeine-pill, thirty-six-hour-study-session kind of person. You need to keep at it on a daily basis so you won't get overwhelmed.

You should give yourself breaks during your study time, too. I'd tell myself, "In ninety minutes I'm going to go out and get a coffee and not take my books" or "In an hour, I'm going to go and work out."

It's wise to find a good balance for yourself early on. Do some homework, get a decent amount of sleep, do some exercise, eat some healthy foods, and give yourself a social or mental break each day.

COLLEGE LIFE

DOROTHY, YOU'RE NOT IN HIGH SCHOOL ANYMORE!

One unrealistic expectation that you may need to shake: don't expect college to be a glorified version of high school. One of the outstanding accomplishments of your high school career may have been how active and well-rounded you were, involved in eight different activities. In high school you may have been a part of everything. You may expect that college will continue to offer that opportunity, but you are failing to appreciate the difference in the academic demands. College classes are challenging. The class work is harder than it was in high school. It takes more time. You won't have time to take a full load and still be involved in a medley of activities.

When I started at Yale, I fully intended to be involved in three or four different clubs and activities, in addition to academics, and I wanted to devote myself to music, too. I joined the marching band and intended to be in concert band, as well.

I quickly realized that studying for class was such a heavy load, I only had time for my class schedule and band.

Starting out, I had a false sense of what was involved in the college experience because I had gone all through grade school and high school on a college campus back home. My K–12 school was a university lab school located right on the campus, so I had witnessed college life firsthand; and toward the end of high school, I even had the opportunity to take some college classes. But witnessing college from that vantage point was not the same as when I was immersed in it.

SETTLING IN

College was drastically different from high school in every imaginable way. For one thing, I was so far from home. Yale is halfway across the country from my hometown, so when I got homesick—and I did get homesick—I couldn't just hop on a train like a lot of my friends and be home in an hour.

The size and diversity of the community required an adjustment, too. My little hometown is a pretty homogenous community, and it's buried in the rural countryside. As you travel east, the closer you get to the East Coast, it's just city after city with no break, no green pastures in between.

The pace is different, too. People are in a flurry of constant activity, doing something all the time.

And Yale was so intimidating because all of my fellow students seemed so brilliant and had such distinguished backgrounds; they all seemed so absolutely qualified to be there. It makes you wonder, "Where do I fit in? Did they make a mistake by accepting me to Yale? Will they figure out that I don't belong in this company, and send me home?"

When I tried to describe my home to people at Yale, it was hard for my fellow students to relate to. Some of them thought of the Midwest as a bunch of "flyover states." In fact, the first time I ever heard that expression was when I was at Yale.

I made friends pretty quickly, but I still missed my family and friends from home. When the academic work became overwhelming, I didn't have my family to see to it that I took a break from the work load. I combated the homesickness by finding activities that I enjoyed and that kept me busy until I could see my family again. I actually got a break every six weeks; either my family would come up to visit or I'd get to go home for a holiday. Some students lived so far away that they couldn't go home at all, which I felt was pretty sad. I needed that time with my family.

MAKING HEALTHY CHOICES

I definitely gained weight my first semester, but I figured out how to adjust my habits to become healthier during the rest of college.

There are always temptations to eat junk in college, but you should try to maintain a well-balanced diet. Eating was a very social activity at Yale; dinners often lasted two hours, and portion control was difficult to maintain in the buffet-style dining halls. Dining halls always offer some sort of healthy option, such as a salad bar, so be aware of those. On the other hand, don't beat yourself up too much over occasional indulgences at the dessert bar.

HOW TO AVOID THE FRESHMAN FIFTEEN

- Maintain a well-balanced diet.
- Avoid junk food.
- Control your portions.
- Make healthy choices, like going to the salad bar.
- Exercise! Make good use of the gym on campus.

I would suggest looking at the gym schedule at the beginning of the year and scheduling some gym classes or workout time into your schedule, just like you do with all of your academic classes. My biggest regret is not establishing an exercise routine at the beginning of my first semester. Once I did start exercising regularly, I was healthier and less stressed, and I got the built-in mental break I so often needed.

FRIENDS AND ROOMMATES

I was lucky; I got along with my roommates most of the time. It's always difficult to share a room with someone who has a different schedule or a different lifestyle than you do. I just tried to be flexible and willing to compromise. I figured I had enough stress at school without constantly picking fights with my roommates.

It wasn't hard to make friends at Yale. So many of us had come from different places, most of us didn't know a lot of people. You just have to put yourself out there; don't be afraid to say hi. Don't be shy. Give people a chance. The people who make a lot of friends quickly aren't smarter, cooler, or better looking than you; they're just willing to meet new people.

> **The people who make friends quickly aren't smarter, cooler, or better looking than you; they're just willing to meet new people.**

Remember to be yourself! Don't try to be someone you're not because you think it will impress other people.

One thing I would do differently if I had it to do over again would be to get to know some people better. There were so many talented and exceptional people to meet. After graduation I moved to Washington, D.C., along with several other Yale graduates. I got to know many of them much better once we were in a different environment, but I wish I would have taken the time to know them better in college.

MEMORABLE EXPERIENCES

Every student at Yale was assigned to a residential college, and each college had a master and a dean—kind of like Hogwarts in the Harry Potter books. The master would hold tea parties each month, inviting not only the residents of the hall, but distinguished people from different backgrounds. It was unbelievable: I had tea with Richard Dreyfuss, with Diane von

Furstenberg; I met ballerinas from the American Ballet Theater, editors from the *New York Times*, and politicians from Washington, D.C.

On top of that, it was a treat just to enjoy all of my fellow students at these teas, and to have the opportunity to talk to them. They were as amazing as the distinguished guests.

SOME WISE ADVICE

There are people who will tell you, "College is the best time of your life," and I do not believe it.

It's a great time and a great experience, but hearing that college is as good as it gets puts pressure on you: you might worry if you're not making perfect grades or perfect relationships or having the time of your life. Trust me, this is not the pinnacle; it's not all downhill from here. Your life is not over at twenty-one!

You should be prepared for an adjustment period when you go to college. I'm sure that most students don't find their first semester to be easy. You should be prepared to make new friends, to be in a new environment, and for classes to be harder than they were in high school.

With that said, you should also look forward to all of the new experiences you will have, and new opportunities that are awaiting you.

AND MOST IMPORTANTLY . . .

Try something new! It's probably a cliché, but college really is the best time to try that hobby or occupation that you were curious about. College is a great time to try something new because there are so many opportunities and resources on and around campuses. College is one of the most flexible times in a person's life; it's a time that's designed for exploration.

> **College is one of the most flexible times in a person's life; it's a time that's designed for exploration.**

Also, don't be afraid of change. Change your major, change your friends, change your hairstyle. If you ever wanted to do something new, college is the time to do it. ★

For more from Kaleen go to
www.nowyoutellmebooks.com/college.

ANGELA WEBBER

ADVICE FROM AN RA
(Residential Adviser)

BONDING WITH HALL MATES

Your hall mates are a good group of people to get to know, and although you'll probably connect with them naturally, it doesn't hurt to reach out to them first.

Your hall can become your home away from home, and your hall mates can become your family.

I had a different experience: freshman year, I was sort of the "odd one out" in my hall. I spent a lot of time away from my dorm, and I felt like everyone got along better without me. Even so, when my birthday rolled around, my neighbor baked me a cake, and everyone joined in to sing and wish me well.

Whatever your experience is, your hall can become your home away from home, and your hall mates can become your family. And, love 'em or hate 'em, you've gotta have a home.

PARTYING

Regardless of what you may think or what the campus tour showed you, you will confront some partying on your campus. But as long as you set some limits for yourself and know what you are and aren't comfortable with, dealing with peer pressure will be a breeze. And if you do choose to party, here are some tips from a RA:

1. **Keep your music at a reasonable volume, stay chill, and keep your door closed.** The last thing you want to do is visibly and obviously break rules. You may want to save the beer pong tournament for an off-campus party and play some rock band instead. Or, whatever you kids are doing these days.

2. **Remember: residence halls are primarily places in which to live, sleep, and study.** They are also places where parties happen, and that is not always approved of. Your campus will have some way of dealing with this—"write-up" and "consequence" systems. You will probably hear people ragging on that RA who wrote them up and ruined their party, but remember, it could always be worse, which brings me to my next tip. . . .

3. **Remember: RAs are there so the cops don't have to be.** A residence hall is a community, and when you're disturbing the peace in that community, something needs to be done. Think about whether your party is disturbing your neighbors and others in your building. Are you making a mess? Are you creating a hazardous situation? Then wouldn't it make sense for it to be stopped?

COLLEGE LIFE

College is hard. It's rough being surrounded by a bunch of like-minded people, when all of these people are wondering: "Did I make the right choice coming here? Should I transfer? Should I have even gone to college?

What should my major be? Will this make me happy? This is hard; why am I paying for this? Am I wasting my life? Will I get a job? Will I ever find a boyfriend or girlfriend? What's the point?"

We're all in the same boat, and we all wonder those things at one point or another. My advice is: get into some sort of routine where you get off campus and can keep your mind from wandering and worrying. Get a job or internship, or just go into town. Meet some people who aren't eighteen-year-olds. It's amazing how quickly you can forget what real people look like. When some professor brings her kid to school, everyone flips out, because we never see children anymore! Or old people!

> **Meet some people who aren't eighteen-year-olds. It's amazing how quickly you can forget what real people look like.**

College is a very weird and unique situation in a lot of ways. Get ready for it. And enjoy.

—Angela Webber, Lewis and Clark College, Portland, Oregon ★

For more from Angela go to
www.nowyoutellmebooks.com/college.

STRESS-FREE TRANSITIONING TO COLLEGE: HOW PARENTS CAN HELP

CAROLINE G. BEISCHER, PSY.D.

When your son or daughter leaves for college—especially if it's your first-born child who is heading out the door—the transition will make a major impact on each member of the family. While the focus is on the college student's adjustment, everyone in the family will have to get used to a different way of being a family. If you are involved in the process and informed about all the options, you will be able to support your son or daughter and cope with the normal shift in your relationship. The information that follows is designed to give you a sense of the issues that will inevitably come up, so that you can be ready to help your child make a successful transition.

ORIENTATION: AN ESSENTIAL PRELUDE

Before college officially begins, make it a priority to attend the college's orientation programs. For students and parents alike, the orientation sessions are the most efficient way to gain information. If possible, attend the first session offered by the school. You will get a jump on college plans, calm anxieties, and select fall courses before other incoming freshman.

COMMUNICATIONS 101

When living under the same roof, you probably gave very little thought to planning communications with your child. However, before college begins, consider laying down some rules and expectations about communications.

For example, you might decide that you expect your son or daughter to check and respond to your e-mails, calls, and text messages promptly. In return, you will commit to keeping your e-mails, calls, and text messages brief and send them only when needed. Depending on your child's level of independence and anxiety, you may need to be in more frequent contact. In any case, you will want to encourage your child to form supportive connections at school, so he or she can let go of you and home with confidence. Sometimes this requires a firm stance about not coming home for the first several months along with a steady flow of positive mail and comforting care packages.

CHANGING ROLES AND EXPECTATIONS

It's a new world. Welcome to the Family Educational Rights and Privacy Act (FERPA). Guess what: according to the FERPA Web site, "Once a student reaches 18 years of age or attends a postsecondary institution, he or she becomes an 'eligible student,' and all rights formerly given to parents under FERPA transfer to the student." Check out the FERPA guidelines at ed.gov/policy/gen/guid/fpco/ferpa/students.html for details. What this really means is that, by law, the college or university will treat your child as an adult. You generally will not have access to information about grades, finances, or other details of college life unless you go through your student. Consequently, you would be wise to have your son or daughter start taking care of his or her college business, including bills, account balances, grades, and any campus problems from the start. In certain situations the college will not even speak to a parent unless the student has signed a FERPA waiver. Check out your institution's policy online.

In reality, your child will lean on you as much as you allow. When he asks you for advice, encourage him to connect with the various resources on campus so he can start to develop confidence and self-reliance. He can get answers just as easily as you can, and then you can help with final decisions if more input is needed.

CAMPUS RESOURCES AND SERVICES: KNOW THEM AND USE THEM

A college campus operates as a self-contained community in many ways, and except for emergencies, most of your child's needs can be met on campus. Departments such as the health clinic, security, psychological services, tutoring, and job/career placement all exist to aid your student while in school. Make sure she understands that "the squeaky wheel gets the grease." She must seek and secure the services and support she needs at the earliest possible stage. If you know your child will have trouble with anxiety and adjustment, make sure she connects with a counselor on campus at the start of her first semester. If she tends to struggle academically in a certain area, make sure she secures tutoring support. If she is entitled to academic or housing accommodations due to a special need, make sure she knows the policy and procedures in advance. Students need to understand that they are essentially customers of the school they attend. The college has a vested interest in their overall satisfaction (and your satisfaction as a parent), as well as in their academic success and degree completion. Helping students is a responsibility of the institution.

EMBRACE YOUR INSTITUTION: OWN IT AND WHAT IT HAS TO OFFER

Each college has a full suite of resources, services, programs, clubs, activities, events, special offers, and opportunities. Together with your son or daughter, learn all that is available by reading and researching the institution's Web site and campus literature. Comb the campus on several occasions. By walking around the student center, administrative offices, and dorms, you will get to know what and where things of importance are located and who handles specific responsibilities. If you don't see what you are looking for, ask someone and don't stop asking until you are satisfied. If you keep hitting a dead end, take it to a high level college administrator. Remember, the college wants you to be satisfied!

GETTING INVOLVED: AN ESSENTIAL PART OF STUDENT LIFE

Connecting with other students, mentors, and campus contacts, and just knowing many friendly faces, helps make adjusting to college more successful. While it may be a struggle for some students, they need to push themselves out of their comfort zone to meet and make friends. After all, everyone is new and a bit scared. Encourage your student to "JUST DO IT"—pick an event or group of interest, show up, participate, and don't be so afraid of what others will think. In the process, your child may make a friend for life.

ACADEMICS: DEMANDS AND SHIFTS TO KEEP IN MIND

Transitioning from high school to college is huge in terms of academic demands. This shift is often underestimated by students and causes unforeseen stress and anxiety. Consider that in high school, students see their teachers over ten months on a daily or every-other-day basis for less than an hour on average. In college, students see their professors once or twice weekly for sessions that range from fifty minutes to two-and-a-half hours. Classes may be at almost any time of the day or night. The semester is only fifteen weeks long, and final grades could be determined by a few important exams. Professors don't always take attendance, and they may never recognize your son or daughter's name or face. It is up to a student to make a point of meeting professors face-to-face, and going to see them during office hours or e-mailing them if there is an issue or concern. Generally, professors are very helpful and interested in a student's success, and your child should not be afraid to approach an instructor. Remember, students are consumers of knowledge, and the more involved they are with thoroughly understanding the course work and their professor's expectations, the more likely they are to attain academic success.

MAINTAINING A HEALTHY, BALANCED SCHEDULE

Along with the changes in academic demands, creating a balanced life may be the most demanding adjustment for a new college student—and perhaps the area of greatest concern as you send your child off into the wider world without you. Even though they will experience many bumps and scrapes in the process, college students need to learn on their own just how much they can manage in every aspect of functioning. Still, it will be important to stress that moderation is the absolute key to success and that self-control and self-discipline will enable them to do what they would rather not do, when they really should. Teach your child how to develop a weekly schedule that includes classes, study time, socializing, campus activities, health maintenance (nutrition, sleep, exercise, stress-reduction), and time alone. Help him or her recognize the signs and dangers of imbalance such as getting sick, feeling overwhelmed, or becoming depressed. Discuss ways to create space and opportunities to be alone on a regular basis as a way to clear the mind, if this is important and helpful for your student to function best.

RELATIONSHIPS AND ROOMMATES

For some students, creating and maintaining relationships with peers and partners comes naturally. For others, this is a challenge and they go off to college with very little experience. Make sure your college-bound student is well informed of appropriate limits and knowledge of "The Golden Rule"—"Do unto others as you would have them do unto you." Remind your child that the residence advisor (RA) is available to help resolve conflicts and enable roommates and dorm-mates to live together in harmony. Know the RAs and use them. Remember, they get paid and/or receive free housing in exchange for helping students.

WISE CHOICES: SEX, DRUGS, AND ALCOHOL

Easy access to, and the opportunity to experiment with, sex, drugs, and alcohol may be a new frontier and a potential risk for an incoming college student. This issue is an even more serious concern if the student has impulse control challenges (ADHD), tries too hard to fit in (social skills' weaknesses), or has a hard time saying "NO" (low self-confidence or self-esteem). Make sure he knows your expectations and limits for appropriate behavior. Remind him that respectable and honorable conduct will keep him out of all sorts of trouble now and in the future. Plus, the college has its own set of rules. If a student crosses a line, he could be expelled. Also, make sure he clearly understands the health and social risks associated with promiscuity and casual/unprotected sex.

FOSTERING TOLERANCE, DIVERSITY, AND AN OPEN MIND

Depending on the location and size of the college, your child is likely to encounter a widely diverse student and faculty population. This may be an unfamiliar situation but serves as a wonderful opportunity to learn about other cultures, values, and traditions. Chances are that after college she will end up in the work world with equally diverse coworkers. Encourage your student to reach out of her comfort zone to meet new and different student populations and to avoid cliques and the same-old, same-old student who looks a lot like her. She may end up meeting her new best friend, the love of her life, or a future business partner.

MONEY MATTERS

Technological advances have made money management on college campuses a breeze. In many cases, your son or daughter's unique student ID card will also be a meal card and campus/local business debit card. The accounts can be monitored and refilled online by the student or parents. You will need to decide on your own what to do about extra spending money for purchases, meals out, etc. Again, explaining to your offspring the limits and expectations for spending before leaving for campus will save future problems and heartache.

SAFETY, SECURITY, AND PERSONAL PROPERTY

College campuses today take student safety very seriously. Emergency "Blue Light Phones" are popping up all over college campuses in an effort to establish an atmosphere of safety and security for all students (and their parents). By simply picking up the phone and pushing one of two buttons, you can be connected to either "911" or a campus transportation dispatcher and possibly get a ride from a security officer if you feel threatened or uncomfortable at any time on campus. Make sure your student knows to keep personal property such as medication, cell phone, computer, and other electronic devices under lock and key or safely within a locked dorm room. And be sure that your child also knows standard rules when traveling alone or in unfamiliar places. If necessary, have your college-bound student take a self-defense course before leaving home to increase personal safety confidence and to give you peace of mind.

Well, that about wraps it up. Expect some bumps and scrapes as you both adjust to increased independence and maturity. Don't overreact. Keep it all in perspective and remember your offspring will grow up a great deal over the next four years. Good luck!

STUFF YOU SHOULD BRING

HOUSEHOLD STUFF

- ❏ Alarm clock (with a snooze button)
- ❏ All-purpose cleaner
- ❏ Bed risers
- ❏ Can/bottle opener
- ❏ Comforter
- ❏ Clothes hangers
- ❏ Dish soap
- ❏ Extra-long twin bed sheets
- ❏ Flashlight and batteries
- ❏ Food storage bags
- ❏ Food storage containers
- ❏ Laundry detergent
- ❏ Laundry basket (collapsible)
- ❏ Microwave-safe mugs and dishes
- ❏ Paper towels
- ❏ Pillows and pillowcases
- ❏ Sponge
- ❏ Tool kit
- ❏ Towels
- ❏ Trash bags
- ❏ Trash bin
- ❏ Travel mug

❏ Utensils
❏ Water bottle

ELECTRONIC STUFF

❏ Cell phone and charger
❏ Ethernet cable
❏ Flash drive
❏ Laptop and laptop charger
❏ Laptop case
❏ Surge protector

SCHOOL STUFF

❏ Backpack
❏ Binders
❏ Calculator
❏ Calendar
❏ College-rule lined paper
❏ Daily planner
❏ Dictionary
❏ Erasers
❏ Highlighters
❏ Notebooks
❏ Notecards
❏ Paper clips and binder clips
❏ Pencil sharpener
❏ Pens and pencils
❏ Pocket folders
❏ Ruler
❏ Scissors
❏ Stapler and staples
❏ Sticky notes
❏ Tape (Scotch, duct)

TOILETRY STUFF

- ❏ Allergy medicine
- ❏ Antacid
- ❏ Bath and hand soap
- ❏ Contacts (and lens case and solution)
- ❏ Cold and cough medicine
- ❏ Dental floss
- ❏ Deodorant
- ❏ First-aid kit
- ❏ Grooming items
  - ☐ Brush or comb
  - ☐ Hair bands and pins
  - ☐ Hair dryer
  - ☐ Nail clippers and file
  - ☐ Razor and shaving cream
  - ☐ Tweezers
- ❏ Hand sanitizer
- ❏ Ibuprofen or other pain-reliever
- ❏ Prescription medications
- ❏ Shampoo and conditioner
- ❏ Toothbrush
- ❏ Toothpaste
- ❏ Vitamins (Flintstones or gummies . . . they're fun to take!)

MISCELLANEOUS STUFF

- ❏ Bank account information
- ❏ Credit/debit card
- ❏ Dress clothes (for special events)
- ❏ Insurance information/medical records
- ❏ Other important documents
- ❏ Student loan information
- ❏ Umbrella

STUFF YOU MAY WANT TO BRING

HOUSEHOLD STUFF

- ❏ Bulletin board
- ❏ Command Strips™ or other adhesive hooks
- ❏ Decorations
- ❏ Desk lamp
- ❏ Desk organizer
- ❏ Doorstop
- ❏ Dry-erase board
- ❏ Drying rack (for laundry)
- ❏ Fan
- ❏ Futon
- ❏ Lint brush
- ❏ Mattress pad
- ❏ Mirror
- ❏ Pictures of family and friends
- ❏ Portable iron and small ironing board
- ❏ Posters
- ❏ Spare light bulbs
- ❏ Stain remover
- ❏ Storage bins
- ❏ Tape measure
- ❏ Water filter pitcher (such as Brita)

ELECTRONIC STUFF

- ❏ Adapters
- ❏ Camera and camera charger
- ❏ CD player/stereo and CDs

- ❏ DVD player and DVDs
- ❏ Extension cords
- ❏ iPod and iPod charger
- ❏ Laptop speakers
- ❏ Mouse and mouse pad
- ❏ Video game console and video games

SCHOOL STUFF

- ❏ Colored markers and pencils
- ❏ Permanent markers
- ❏ Printer
  - ☐ Printer paper
  - ☐ Printer ink cartridges
- ❏ Rubber bands
- ❏ Thesaurus
- ❏ Three-hole punch
- ❏ Thumbtacks/pushpins
- ❏ White-out

TOILETRY STUFF

- ❏ Curling or straightening iron
- ❏ Fragrance (cologne or perfume)
- ❏ Make-up
- ❏ Mouthwash
- ❏ Nail polish and remover
- ❏ Shower caddy
- ❏ Shower shoes
- ❏ Sunscreen
- ❏ Tissues

MISCELLANEOUS STUFF

- ☐ Address book
- ☐ Bike and bike lock
- ☐ Board games
- ☐ Lip balm
- ☐ Mailing envelopes
- ☐ Playing cards
- ☐ Postage stamps
- ☐ Raingear (boots and coat)
- ☐ Religious texts
- ☐ Rolls of quarters (for laundry, vending machines, etc.)
- ☐ Sewing repair kit
- ☐ Sports equipment
- ☐ Sunglasses
- ☐ Swim goggles
- ☐ Swimsuit
- ☐ Umbrella

STUFF TO DISCUSS WITH YOUR ROOMMATE

- ☐ Area rug
- ☐ CD player/stereo and CDs
- ☐ Coffeemaker
- ☐ DVD player and DVDs
- ☐ Hot plate
- ☐ Hot pot
- ☐ Microwave
- ☐ Mini refrigerator
- ☐ Television

❏ Toaster oven
❏ Vacuum (small and lightweight)

STUFF TO LEAVE AT HOME

❏ Autographed picture of Darth Vader
❏ Expensive jewelry or other valuables
❏ Karaoke machine
❏ Out-of-season clothing
❏ Pets

To help you further prepare for your college experience, visit www.NowYouTellMeBooks.com/college for more comprehensive lists.

ABOUT THE AUTHORS

SHERIDAN SCOTT, the primary author of the *Now You Tell Me!* series, has edited half a dozen *Chicken Soup for the Soul* books as well as serving as an author. An award winning biographer, she has been a staff writer for five national magazines, and has ghostwritten for dozens of celebrities, as well as hundreds of regular folks.

ANYA SETTLE, a recent graduate holding a B.A. in English with a minor in creative writing, has contributed poems and short stories to the *Dickinson Review,* and has participated as a student poet in the international Semana Poética poetry festival. Anya currently works in communications by day, and works as a freelance writer and editor in her spare time. She lives outside New York City.

NANCY ALLEN is a member of the law faculty in the College of Business Administration at Missouri State University, where she obtained her undergraduate degree. After graduating from University of Missouri School of Law, Nancy served as Assistant Missouri Attorney General for nine years, and as Assistant Prosecutor in her native Ozarks for five years. Nancy lives in Southwest Missouri with her husband and two children. She is a regular contributor to the *Real Estate Law Journal,* and she is currently working on a novel.

Would you like a mentor? If so visit
www.nowyoutellmebooks.com/college
and join the conversation.